First World War
and Army of Occupation
War Diary
France, Belgium and Germany

63 (ROYAL NAVAL) DIVISION
188 Infantry Brigade,
Brigade Machine Gun Company
31 July 1916 - 28 February 1918

WO95/3111/4

The Naval & Military Press Ltd
www.nmarchive.com
Published in association with The National Archives

Published by

The Naval & Military Press Ltd

Unit 10 Ridgewood Industrial Park,

Uckfield, East Sussex,

TN22 5QE England

Tel: +44 (0) 1825 749494

www.naval-military-press.com

www.nmarchive.com

This diary has been reprinted in facsimile from the original. Any imperfections are inevitably reproduced and the quality may fall short of modern type and cartographic standards.

© Crown Copyright
Images reproduced by permission of The National Archives, London, England, 2015.

Contents

Document type	Place/Title	Date From	Date To
Heading	WO95/3111-4		
Heading	63rd Division 188th Infy Bde No.188th Machine Gun Coy Aug 1916-Feb 1918		
Miscellaneous	Reference Sheet	01/09/1916	01/09/1916
War Diary		31/07/1916	29/09/1916
War Diary	La Corte	02/10/1916	03/10/1916
War Diary	Sibiville	04/10/1916	04/10/1916
War Diary	La Comte	04/10/1916	05/10/1916
War Diary	Ligny St Flochel	05/10/1916	05/10/1916
War Diary	Varennes	05/10/1916	05/10/1916
War Diary	Englebelmer	05/10/1916	19/10/1916
War Diary	Varennes	20/10/1916	20/10/1916
War Diary	Englebelmer	20/10/1916	06/11/1916
War Diary	Puchevillers	06/11/1916	06/11/1916
War Diary	Hedauville	06/11/1916	07/11/1916
War Diary	Englebelmer	07/11/1916	09/11/1916
War Diary	('W' Day)	10/11/1916	10/11/1916
War Diary	('X' Day)	11/11/1916	11/11/1916
War Diary	('Y' Day)	12/11/1916	12/11/1916
War Diary	(Z Day)	13/11/1916	30/11/1916
Miscellaneous	Appendix "C" Orders for 188th Machine Gun Company	09/11/1916	09/11/1916
War Diary	Hamelet	01/12/1916	11/12/1916
War Diary	Arry	12/12/1916	17/12/1916
War Diary	Lannoy	18/12/1916	28/12/1916
War Diary	Rue	29/12/1916	15/01/1917
War Diary	G.R. Mont	16/01/1917	17/01/1917
War Diary	Beauquesne	18/01/1917	18/01/1917
War Diary	Englebelmer	19/01/1917	31/01/1917
War Diary	Thiepval	31/01/1917	28/02/1917
Miscellaneous	Appendix "A" Action by 188th and 190th Machine Gun Companies	15/02/1917	15/02/1917
War Diary	Martinsart	02/03/1917	02/03/1917
War Diary	Bouzincourt	02/03/1917	27/03/1917
War Diary	Noeux-Les-Mines	28/03/1917	30/04/1917
Heading	War Diary of 223rd Machine Gun Company From 1st May 1917 To 31st May 1917 Volume II		
War Diary	Ourton Pas De Calais	01/05/1917	05/05/1917
War Diary	Magnicourt-En-Comte	06/05/1917	08/05/1917
War Diary	Villers Brulin	09/05/1917	11/05/1917
War Diary	Roclincourt	12/05/1917	20/05/1917
War Diary	STE. Catherine	20/05/1917	31/05/1917
Operation(al) Order(s)	Relief Order No.1 By Captain J.B. Dodge D.S.C. Commanding 223rd Machine Gun Company	30/05/1917	30/05/1917
Heading	War Diary of 188th Machine Gun Company From 1st June 1917 To 30th June 1917 Volume III		
War Diary	Sainte Catherine	01/06/1917	03/06/1917
War Diary	Trenches	03/06/1917	03/06/1917
War Diary	B 28a5.8	04/06/1917	04/06/1917
War Diary	Trenches B 28.a.5.8.	05/06/1917	12/06/1917

Type	Description	Start	End
War Diary	Maroeuil	12/06/1917	30/06/1917
Operation(al) Order(s)	Relief Order No.2 By Captain J.B. Dodge D.S.C. Commanding 225 Machine Gun Company	09/06/1917	09/06/1917
Heading	War Diary of 188th Machine Gun Company From 1st June 1917 To 30th June 1917 Volume III		
War Diary	Sainte Catherine	01/06/1917	03/06/1917
War Diary	Trenches B 28a 5.8	04/06/1917	12/06/1917
War Diary	Maroeuil	12/06/1917	30/06/1917
Miscellaneous	Relief Order No.2	09/06/1917	09/06/1917
Heading	War Diary of 188th Machine Gun Company From 1st July 1917 To 31st July 1917 Volume No.		
Miscellaneous	Subject Duplicate War Diaries	23/09/1917	23/09/1917
Miscellaneous	188 Machine Gun Company	08/10/1917	08/10/1917
Miscellaneous	To Secret A.G.'s Officer 3rd Echelon	25/08/1917	25/08/1917
War Diary	Maroeuil	01/07/1917	03/07/1917
War Diary	Ste. Catherine	04/07/1917	05/07/1917
War Diary	Trenches Coy H.Q At HIc 7.4	05/07/1917	08/07/1917
War Diary	Trenches	08/07/1917	31/07/1917
Operation(al) Order(s)	No.188 Machine Gun Company Operation Order No.3	03/07/1917	03/07/1917
Operation(al) Order(s)	No.188 Machine Gun Company Operation Order No.4	07/07/1917	07/07/1917
Operation(al) Order(s)	No.188 M.G. Company Operation Order No.5	16/07/1917	16/07/1917
Operation(al) Order(s)	No.188th Machine Gun Company Operation Order No.6	20/07/1917	20/07/1917
Operation(al) Order(s)	188th M.G Coy. Operation Order No.7	22/07/1917	22/07/1917
Operation(al) Order(s)	Relief Order No.8		
Heading	War Diary of 188th Machine Gun Company From 1st Aug 1917 To 1917 Volume No.4		
War Diary	West Roclincourt Camp	01/08/1917	08/08/1917
War Diary	Trenches	08/08/1917	25/08/1917
War Diary	West Roclincourt Camp	26/08/1917	31/08/1917
Operation(al) Order(s)	188 Machine Gun Company Relief Order No.9	07/08/1917	07/08/1917
Operation(al) Order(s)	No 188 Machine Gun Company Operation Order No.10		
Operation(al) Order(s)	No 188 Machine Gun Company Operation Order No.11		
Operation(al) Order(s)	No 188 Machine Gun Company Operation Order No.12		
Operation(al) Order(s)	No 188 Machine Gun Company Operation Order No.13		
Heading	War Diary of 188 Machine Gun Company From Sep 1st 1917 To Sep 30th 1917		
War Diary	Roclincourt	01/09/1917	02/09/1917
War Diary	Trenches	03/09/1917	19/09/1917
War Diary	St. Aubin	20/09/1917	30/09/1917
Operation(al) Order(s)	No.188 Machine Gun Company Operation Order No.14		
Operation(al) Order(s)	No.188 Machine Gun Company Operation Order No.15	10/09/1917	10/09/1917
Operation(al) Order(s)	188 Machine Gun Company Operation Order No.16		
Operation(al) Order(s)	188 Machine Gun Company Operation Order No.17	21/09/1917	21/09/1917
Heading	188 Machine Gun Company War Diary From Oct 1st 1917 To Oct 31/1917		
War Diary	Monchy Breton	01/10/1917	02/10/1917
War Diary	Poperinghe	02/10/1917	02/10/1917
War Diary	Dirty Bucket Camp	03/10/1917	03/10/1917
War Diary	P Camp	09/10/1917	22/10/1917
War Diary	Trish Farm	23/10/1917	26/10/1917
War Diary	Trish Farm Camp	27/10/1917	31/10/1917
Heading	War Diary 188 M.Gun Company From Nov 1st 1917 To 30th 1917		
War Diary	Dambre Camp	01/11/1917	05/11/1917
War Diary	Line	06/11/1917	06/11/1917

War Diary	Irish-Farm	07/11/1917	07/11/1917
War Diary	School Camp	08/11/1917	11/11/1917
War Diary	Winnezeele	12/11/1917	12/11/1917
War Diary	Ledringham	13/11/1917	25/11/1917
War Diary	Dambre Camp	26/11/1917	30/11/1917
Heading	War Diary 188 MG Coy To 31st Dec 1917 Vol 20		
War Diary	Line D 4d7 9	01/12/1917	03/12/1917
War Diary	Dambre Camp	04/12/1917	05/12/1917
War Diary	Schools Camp	06/12/1917	08/12/1917
War Diary	Beaulen-Court N. 18.a	09/12/1917	13/12/1917
War Diary	Rocquigny	14/12/1917	14/12/1917
War Diary	Manancourt	15/12/1917	15/12/1917
War Diary	Lechelle	16/12/1917	16/12/1917
War Diary	In The Line	25/12/1917	31/12/1917
War Diary	Lechelle	16/12/1917	21/12/1917
War Diary	Metz	22/12/1917	24/12/1917
Heading	188 Coy M.G.C. War Diary from 1st to 31st January 1918		
War Diary	In The Line	01/01/1918	09/01/1918
War Diary	Metz	10/01/1918	16/01/1918
War Diary	In The Line	17/01/1918	24/01/1918
War Diary	Equancourt	24/01/1918	24/01/1918
War Diary	Rocquigny	25/01/1918	13/02/1918
War Diary	Havrincourt Wood	14/02/1918	28/02/1918

8095/3111(4)

63RD DIVISION
188TH INFY BDE

NO. 188TH MACHINE GUN COY

AUG 1916-FEB 1918

63RD DIVISION
188TH INFY BDE

S.—546. (Revised—October, 1899.)
D.—398.

REFERENCE SHEET.

From __O.C.__

His Majesty's __188th Machine Gun Coy.__

To __Headquarters,__
__188th Brigade.__

at _____

Dated __1st September__ 1916..

Information required, or notified

Submitted.
Enclosed is copy of War Diary Volume III for the month
of August 1916.

A. Bennett.
Lieut. R.N.V.R.
O.C.

188th Machine Gun Company

Army Form C. 2118.

Vol 1

WAR DIARY
or
INTELLIGENCE SUMMARY.
(Erase heading not required.)

Hour, Date, Place	Summary of Events and Information	Remarks and references to Appendices
1916.		
31. July. 1. Aug.	1.0 a.m. Left GRANTHAM. Embarked SOUTHAMPTON on H.M.T. N.W. MILLER. noon. Arrived LE HAVRE. Proceeding to Rest Camp No. II. where Company remained for the night.	
3. Aug.	1.0 a.m. Left by train for ROUEN and arrived 7.30 a.m. Entrained 4.30 p.m.	
4. Aug.	11.45 a.m. Arrived at BARLIN. Marched to FOSSE X, when transport was billeted, the remainder of the Company proceeding to BILLETS in BULLY-GRENAY. Head Quarters 2 Rue de la Chapelle.	
5th & 6 Aug.	The Officers of the Company inspected the gun positions in the ANGRES Section preparatory to taking over.	
7 Aug.	Three Sections (12 guns) relieved 1 Section (4 guns) of the 189th M.G.C. in the left forward Sub-division, & 1 gun of the Lovats Regiment in the right forward Sub-division and 1 Section 4 guns of the King Edwards Horse in the BAJOLLE Line. One section remained in BILLETS. The 189th Machine Gun Coy. were in the evening relieved by 8 men from 1st R.M.L.I. 8 men from 2nd R.M.L.I. 8 from "Anson" & 8 from "Howe" Battalions were transferred to the Company. Sections were informed that in the event of 51st being relieved in the ANGRES section, all guns were to be withdrawn from the front line. Guns infavourable are not released.	
9 Aug.		
10 Aug.		
13. Aug.	Guns withdrawn from firing line in anticipation of guns being relieved. Wind unfavourable. Guns returned to firing Line.	
18 Aug.	Major Sketchley examined positions and ordered a new emplacement to be constructed at junction of COOKER and SPINNEY Trenches to cover the road in front of COOKER Track.	

188ᵗʰ Machine Gun Coy.

Army Form C. 2118.

WAR DIARY
INTELLIGENCE SUMMARY

(Erase heading not required.)

Instructions regarding War Diaries and Intelligence Summaries are contained in F.S. Regs., Part II and the Staff Manual respectively. Title pages will be prepared in manuscript.

Hour, Date, Place	Summary of Events and Information	Remarks and references to Appendices
21. Aug. 1916. 10.30 pm	Guns relieved. All guns withdrawn from the firing line. One man wounded through BULLY being shelled.	
22. Aug.	A shell struck the gun emplacement in the firing line 20 yards N. of RICHARD TRENCH, wounding 1 man.	
23. Aug.	The above gun was relieved by a Lewis Gun and taken to a new emplacement 15 yards N. of the junction of PIRENEES and BULLY.	
26. Aug.	The gun at VASSEAU trench removed to new emplacement at junction of COOKER and SPINNEY trenches. 2nd lt. gun in front line of left Sub division transferred to new position 20 yards S. of junction of FORREST and BULLY alley. Headquarters of Company and one section transferred to FOSSE X. Headquarters at Stores No. 11.	
29. Aug.	No firing was done by day during the month, but indirect fire was carried out most nights on ration dumps and trenches in the enemy's lines.	

A Bennett Lt. R.N.V.R.

WAR DIARY
INTELLIGENCE SUMMARY
(Erase heading not required.)

Army Form C. 2118.
Vol 2

168

Abbott T. Lieut RNVR

Hour, Date, Place 1916.	Summary of Events and Information	Remarks and references to Appendices
1st September	A.B. Bradshaw proceeded to Trawlers Course at ABBEVILLE.	
3rd "	A.B. Jenkins slightly wounded while at station duty at gun position at junction of SPINNEY and COOKER ALLEY. A.B. Riley transferred to Base until fit.	
4th "	Sub.Lt. R.J. Ranby and 3 men proceeded to Machine Gun Course at CINNIERS.	
8th "	Headquarters transferred from FOSSE X to No. 3 Rue de la Chapelle, BULLY GRENAY. The section in Reserve also removed from FOSSE X to BULLY GRENAY. One reinforcement received.	
11th "	Gun emplacement in PYRENEES damaged by small H.E. Shell. Direct hit on emplacement in NORRON trench. The traverse was badly damaged. One man received no reinforcements.	
15th "	A new position for night firing was constructed at M. 26. C.6.6.	
16th "	The company who withdrawals from the sector ANGRES I & II being relieved by the 112th Machine Gun Company and proceeded to FOSSE X.	
19th "	Sub.Lt. R.J. Ranby transferred to England. Between the 1st & 19th 5920 rounds were fired by night along enemy communication trenches. By day much work was carried out at the gun positions, also dugouts and tracks in the vicinity, many new floor boards being laid and drains dug.	
20th "	The Company left FOSSE X and went into billets at LA COMTE arriving there at 3.00 p.m.	
21st "	Kit inspection and cleaning guns. 2 Officers and 6 N.C.O.'s attended lecture at OURTON on small Box respirator.	
22nd "	Company training.	
23rd "	Do.	
24th "	Do.	
25th "	Do.	
26th "	Brigade training.	
27th "	Do.	
28th "	Divisional training.	
29th "	Divisional Kit & transport.	Sub.Lt. D. Rantzen proceeded to OURTON for 3-day Course 3 men returned from Machine Gun Course at CAMIERS.

188th Machine Gun Coy.
Army Form C. 2118.
Vol 3
Volume V

WAR DIARY
or
INTELLIGENCE SUMMARY.
(Erase heading not required.)

Hour, Date, Place	Summary of Events and Information	Remarks and references to Appendices
2. Oct. La Bonté	Company training.	
3. Oct. "	2nd Lieut. Veal joined Company in place of 2nd Lieut. Rigby, transferred to England.	
7.15am 3 Oct.	4 men Ebting, mules & costs carts + transport, 18 men under 2nd Lieut. Montague, proceeded to Brieulles aut-Bonvilles where the party joined Divisional transport Column and proceeded to Sibiville arriving there at 5 pm. T. billeted for the night.	
8.0 am 4 Oct. Sibiville	The above column marched via FRÉVENT, ETRÉE WAMIN, LUCHEUX, POMMERA, BERTRANCOURT, MAILLY to ENGLEBELMER, arriving there at 4 am Oct. 5.	
9.15 am 4 Oct. La Bonté	C.R.O. Party an 26 men proceeded to Ligny St. Hochel via Auxey. this party entrained at 10.0am arriving at Acheux at 6.0am and marched to billets at ENGLEBELMER.	
1.0 am 5 Oct. La Bonté	8 Officers, 130 men and 8 limbers proceeded to Ligny St Hochel via Auxey.	
3.50 am 5 Oct. Ligny St Hochel	arrived at station.	
8.0 am 5 "	left by train.	
5.15 pm 5 " Varennes.	arrived + detrained.	
9.30 pm 5 " Englebelmer	Men into billets.	
10 am 7 "	Transport moved into billets at Somerville.	
12.45 pm 8 "	Company left and marched to Varennes where they occupied huts.	
8. Oct — 19. Oct. Varennes.		
1.30 pm 19. Oct.	Two gun crews took over positions in BEAUMONT St lts newly front. Aethé.	
1.45 pm. VARENNES. 20. Oct.	left for ENGLEBELMER.	
4.0 pm ENGLEBELMER. 20th	arrived and went into billets.	
11.30 pm–5 am 20/21 Oct.	2300 rounds fired from position at R.19.c.5.2 on station in Q.13.c and Railway Road.	

WAR DIARY or **INTELLIGENCE SUMMARY.**
(Erase heading not required.)

Army Form C. 2118.

Instructions regarding War Diaries and Intelligence Summaries are contained in F.S. Regs., Part II. and the Staff Manual respectively. Title pages will be prepared in manuscript.

Hour, Date, Place	Summary of Events and Information	Remarks and references to Appendices
21. Oct. 1916.	2nd Kent Shirrright, 5th D.L.I. attacks M.G.C. joined the Company no Divisional Official, via SMG line. No runner. R.A.M.C.	
Mid-5am 21/22 Oct.	1750 rounds fired from Q.23.a.6.9. on STATION in Q.18.b. and along RAILWAY ROAD and STATION ROAD. 2nd Lieut. Richards and two guns crews relieved Lieut. Pollet.	
22. Oct.	400 rounds fired from Q.23.a.6.9 on STATION in Q.18.b.	
8.30pm-11.30pm 22. Oct.	Lieut. Pollet and two gun crews were into the line making 4 guns in all	
23. Oct.	4000 rounds fired on STATION, STATION ROAD and RAILWAY ROAD.	
23/24 Oct.	2nd Lieut Reed and 2 guns crew took up position in CHARLES AVENUE	
24. Oct.	above Q.23.a.5.4. making 6 guns in line.	
6pm-5am 24/25 Oct.	7,700 rounds fired on STATION, STATION ROAD, STATION ALLEY and REDOUBT ALLEY.	
	From the 22nd - 24th the remainder of the Company was employed in storing ammunition in dumps in the Trenches.	
25. Oct.	Lieut. Patten and 4 guns crews relieved Lieut. Mellin in CARNALEA (28mm) RNT2L (28mm) SHOOTERS HILL and OLD FRENCH TRENCH.	
6pm-5am 25/26 Oct.	5000 rounds fired on STATION, STATION ROAD and enemy's communication trenches in Q.12.a, C & a.	
10.5-10.45pm 26. Oct.	During the raid by the Yorks Batln. on the enemy's front line at Q.17.b.3.1. three guns traversed the German front line trench between Q.17.b.7.1 & Q.18.a.2.9. (3000 rounds.) 1 gun fired 1000 rounds at suspected M.Gun emplacement at Q.17.b.9.1. and 3000 rounds on the STATION and REDOUBT ALLEY.	

WAR DIARY
INTELLIGENCE SUMMARY
(Erase heading not required.)

Army Form C. 2118.

Hour, Date, Place 1916.	Summary of Events and Information	Remarks and references to Appendices
6.pm - 11.pm Oct. 27.	750 rounds fired on the STATION, 2000 rounds on STATION ROAD, 1000 rounds on ENGINE ALLEY, 1000 rounds on REDOUBT ALLEY and 1000 on STATION ALLEY.	
6.pm - 11.pm Oct. 28.	3000 rounds fired on STATION, STATION ROAD & communication trenches. Bat. Pier. C. Davidson. R.H.V.R. joined the Company.	
" 29	2nd. Lieut. Hamilton & 2nd. Section relieved Lieut Kayn & 3rd section	
6.pm - 11.pm " 29	3000 rounds fired on STATION, STATION ROAD and communication trenches.	
" 30	All positions in the line taken over by the 190th Machine Gun Company.	

A Bennett
T. Lt. R.A. v.c.
O.C.

188th Machine Gun Coy.
Volume III
Vol 4

Army Form C. 2118.

WAR DIARY
or
INTELLIGENCE SUMMARY.
(Erase heading not required.)

Instructions regarding War Diaries and Intelligence Summaries are contained in F.S. Regs., Part II and the Staff Manual respectively. Title pages will be prepared in manuscript.

Hour, Date, Place	Summary of Events and Information	Remarks and references to Appendices
Nov. 1st – 4th 1916	ENGLEBELMER.	
5th 10 a.m	Left ENGLEBELMER for PUCHEVILLERS arriving 3.30 p.m Lieut. Bennett sick. Lieut MacGeorge appointed to take over Command.	
6th 2 pm PUCHEVILLERS	Left for HEDAUVILLE.	
6 pm HEDAUVILLE	Arrived and went into tents.	
7 8.15 am HEDAUVILLE	Left for ENGLEBELMER.	
10.30 am ENGLEBELMER	Arrived. Six guns took over LEFT Sub Section, 2 guns in CARNALEA one in SHOOTERS HILL, one in OLD FRENCH TRENCH and 2 in CHARLES AVENUE. 2000 rounds fired during night 7th/8th on STATION ROAD, RAILWAY ROAD, ENGINE ALLEY & STATION ALLEY	
8.	6 guns relieved by 189th Machine Gun Coy.	
9. 12. noon. ENGLEBELMER.	Inspection by billets by A.O.C. 2nd Division.	
10. (W day)	6 guns relieved 189th Machine Gun Coy in LEFT Sub sector as above.	
11. (X day)	During night 11/12 6600 rounds fired on enemy approaches and communication trenches.	
12. (Y day)	The remaining guns took up their assembly positions by 11 a.m as follows :- Sub Lieut Hamilton with 4 guns near junction of ROBERTS TRENCH and BEDFORD STREET with HOWE Battn., Sub Lt Davison with 2 guns near junction of BEDFORD STREET and VICTORIA STREET and Lieut Mayne with 4 guns near junction of ROBERTS TRENCH and LONG SAP. O.C. with Headquarters 2nd Division in ST JAMES STREET. During the night 12/13 indirect fire was carried out on enemy communication trenches.	
13 (Z day) 5.45 am	Barrage opened and attack commenced, machine guns advancing in accordance with attached appendix.	Appendix "C" marked no I.

(73989) W4141—463. 400,000. 9/14. H.&J.Ltd. Forms/C. 2118/10.

WAR DIARY
or
INTELLIGENCE SUMMARY.
(Erase heading not required.)

Army Form C. 2118.

Instructions regarding War Diaries and Intelligence Summaries are contained in F.S. Regs., Part II. and the Staff Manual respectively. Title pages will be prepared in manuscript.

Hour, Date, Place 1916.	Summary of Events and Information	Remarks and references to Appendices
Apr. 13 (continued.)	The section on the right front was heavily fired on by hostile Machine Guns. The Section Officer who seemed to enter the German front line in advance of his section and was not seen again. Three gun crews were put out of action and the remaining guns crews being relieved by casualties lay in shell holes for 8 hours and eventually joined up with another section. The 3rd Section which advanced with the 1st or Royal Marines owing to the darkness and their mist went too far North. They came into action against a party of German bombers in the front line trench with success. Both section Officers were wounded soon after. The section advanced towards Y ravine. Here 3 guns were put out of action, the 4th under Petty Officer Elliott, pushed forward with the troops line and kept his gun in action until relieved on the 15th. The 1st Section which carried out indirect fire during the advance to the first objective, after refilling the belts faded forward at 6.30am to the S. of Y ravine and came into action against German Machine Guns with success. When the guns were silenced, this section went along the German second line on being informed by hostile acting point about Q.17.b.3.4. Taking up position about 12 noon a heavy fire was brought to bear on the German guns in order to facilitate the advance of the infantry. The 4th Section which also carried out indirect fire during the advance to the first objective pushed forward to the German front line about 8 a.m. in attempting to advance beyond they were met by heavy Machine gun fire and were unable to go forward. During the night 13/14th three from guns came into action just E. to the German front line and carried out indirect fire on the enemy's communication trenches, forming a strong point in case the	

WAR DIARY or INTELLIGENCE SUMMARY.

Army Form C. 2118.

Hour, Date, Place		Summary of Events and Information	Remarks and references to Appendices
Nov. 13. 1916	(Continued)	infantry were forced to retire.	
14.		At dawn the infantry advanced to the GREEN line and 1 gun of the Unit went forward with them and 1 gun of the 190th Machine Gun Coy. which had been placed near the church of L.S. Hollebeke of this Unit. In the afternoon after the capitulation of the German strong point the M.G. section advanced to the German 2nd line. Casualties: Officers. 1 missing. 3 wounded. Other Ranks:- 5 Killed, wounded and missing.	
15.	3.30 p.m.	Relief completed.	
	6.30 p.m.	Arrived HEDAUVILLE.	
16.	4.0 a.m.	Left HEDAUVILLE for PUCHEVILLERS and went into billets.	
		Transport left HEDAUVILLE for PUCHEVILLERS in motor buses, arrived 6 a.m.	
17.	1.30 p.m.	Left for GEZAINCOURT arriving there 1 p.m.	
18.	10.20 a.m.	Left for BEAUMETZ arriving there 2.0 p.m.	
20.	10.30 a.m.	Addressed by G.O.C. Division at BERNAVILLE	
21.	10.15 a.m.	Left for HANCHY arriving there 12.15 p.m.	
22.	10.15 a.m.	Left for DOMVAST arriving there 12. noon. Billeting Party 1 Officer + 1 N.C.O. sent forward to reconnoitre billeting area.	
	10. 0 a.m.		
23.	10.25 a.m.	Left for NOUVION-EN-PONTHIEU arriving there 12.30 p.m.	
24.	10.30 a.m.	Left for BECQUERELLE arriving there at 1.30 p.m.	
26.	11. 0 a.m.	Left for LE HAMELET and went into rest billets.	
27.		Lieut Bennett assumed command	
27-30.		Refitting the Company.	

(Signed) A. Bennett
T/Lt. R.M.V.R.
O.C. 188th M.G.C.

No. I

APPENDIX "C"

ORDERS FOR

188th. Machine Gun Company.

Distribution.	1. Four guns will advance with each Front Line Battalion. Six guns will cover the advance to the first objective with indirect fire from the line CARNALEA-SHOOTERS HILL-OLD FRENCH TRENCH. On the first objective being gained those six guns and the remaining two guns will follow the Support Battalions to the second objective.
Object.	2. All guns must be pushed boldly forward, and come into action in close support of the Battalions with which they advance. The Left flank of the Brigade must be carefully protected. Section Officers in the Left Sub-section on reaching their objective should endeavour to obtain position from which the Left flank of each successive advance may be covered. On arriving at the final objective all guns available must cover all approaches and the flanks of the Brigade, should the advance on the flanks be held up.
Hostile Strong Points.	3. Should these be encountered, Machine Guns should be detailed to cover them.
Assembly.	4. On "Y" day four guns in support of the Howe Battalion will be close to the junction of ROBERTS TRENCH and BEDFORD STREET, four guns in support of 1st. Royal Marines near the junction of ROBERTS TRENCH and LONG SAP, two guns near the junction of BEDFORD STREET and VICTORIA STREET. Officer Commanding Machine Gun Company to arrange with Officer Commanding Battalions concerned.
Headquarters.	5. Headquarters will be attached to Anson Battalion.
Personnel.	6. 32 men will be attached as Ammunition carriers (two per gun). These will report on the evening of "X" day as laid down in Assembly Orders.

Captain,
Brigade Major,
188th. Infantry Brigade.

9-11-16.

188th Machine Gun Company.

Army Form C. 2118.

Volume VII.

WAR DIARY
or
INTELLIGENCE SUMMARY.
(*Erase heading not required.*)

Hour, Date, Place	Summary of Events and Information	Remarks and references to Appendices
1916.		
Dec. 1st - 11th HAMELET.	Sectional Training.	
12th - 17th ARRY.	do.	
18th - 28th LANNOY.	do.	
29th - 31st RUE.	do.	

W. Bennett
Lieut. R.N.R.

Army Form C. 2118.

189th Machine Gun Coy.

Vol 6 Volume VIII

WAR DIARY
of
INTELLIGENCE SUMMARY.
(Erase heading not required.)

Instructions regarding War Diaries and Intelligence Summaries are contained in F. S. Regs., Part II. and the Staff Manual respectively. Title pages will be prepared in manuscript.

Place	Date	Hour	Summary of Events and Information	Remarks and references to Appendices
RUE.	1916/17 1 Jan to 11 Jan		Company training.	
"	11 Jan		O.C. to hospital. Advance party, 1 officer & 2 N.C.O's proceeded to R. line.	
"	12 Jan		Left RUE arrived FOREST L'ABBAYE.	
"	13 Jan		Left FOREST L'ABBAYE arrived DOMVAST.	
"	14 Jan		Left DOMVAST arrived GRIMONT.	
"	15 Jan			
GRIMONT.	16 Jan		Resting.	
"	17 Jan		Left GRIMONT arrived BEAUQUESNE.	
BEAUQUESNE	18 Jan		Left BEAUQUESNE arrived ENGLEBELMER.	
ENGLEBELMER.	19 Jan	2.30 pm	Left ENGLEBELMER and proceeded via MARTINSART and MESNIL and AUTHUILLE to THIEPVAL.	
		7.30 pm	Relieved 33rd M.G.Cy. in Sector S of the ANCRE, taking over 2 guns in BATTERY VALLEY, 4 guns in HANSA LINE, and 4 guns in YELLOW LINE. Headquarters and 4 guns in Reserve established in THIEPVAL at R.25.d.6.2. Transport and Q.M. Stores remained at ENGLEBELMER.	
	20 Jan to 21 Jan	2.30 pm	O.C. returned to duty. During this period the enemy's trenches in front of GRANDCOURT, roads, and approaches to GRANDCOURT have been kept under fire from dusk to midnight and also at dawn.	

Army Form C. 2118.

WAR DIARY

~~INTELLIGENCE~~ SUMMARY.

(Erase heading not required.)

Instructions regarding War Diaries and Intelligence Summaries are contained in F. S. Regs., Part II. and the Staff Manual respectively. Title pages will be prepared in manuscript.

Place	Date	Hour	Summary of Events and Information	Remarks and references to Appendices
	1917.			
THIEPVAL	Jany 31.	10.40pm	During a Battalion relief "S.O.S." signal was sent up, and section in reserve stood to arms.	
"	"	11.40pm	"S.O.S." Cancelled.	

W M Macgeorge J. Capt. H.L.I.
Acting O.C.
188th Machine Gun Coy.

Army Form C. 2118.

188th Machine Gun Coy

Vol VIII

WAR DIARY
or
INTELLIGENCE SUMMARY.
(Erase heading not required.)

Place	Date 1917	Hour	Summary of Events and Information	Remarks and references to Appendices
	1 Feb			
	2 "			
	3 "	11.0.p.m	The Brigade on left attacked PUISIEUX and RIVER trenches N. of the ANCRE from ARTILLERY ALLEY to the river. In conjunction with this operation fire was kept up on BAILLESCOURT FARM and roads in and approaches to GRANDCOURT.	
	4 "		During the day and night bursts of fire were maintained on the above targets, rapid fire being opened during counter attacks by the enemy. In connection with the above operations 41,250 rounds were fired.	
	6 "		O.G. 1 & 2 were occupied without opposition.	
	7 "		During the morning 1 company of the Marines advanced without opposition to the road in R.9.d. and consolidated. The enemy were seen digging in on the ridge running through R.10.a.& c.	
		12 noon	Two guns under Sacrifice Bikes were pushed forward from the YELLOW LINE along the Valley of the ANCRE into GRANDCOURT. Owing to heavy shelling it was found impossible to man the guns in daylight. At night the guns were established at R.15.a.9.7.	
		11.0.pm	The Brigade on the left attacked the road running S.E. to N.W. in R.3.C. and BAILLESCOURT FARM.	
	8 "	1.30 am	The Brigade in the night attacked and held FOLLY trench in R.16.C. The two remaining guns in YELLOW LINE were withdrawn and two from the HANSA LINE.	
	9 "		2 guns were pushed forward into O.G.1. The line now being held with 2 guns in GRANDCOURT, 2 guns in O.G.1. 1 gun in BATTERY VALLEY, 1 gun in STUFF trench and 2 guns in HANSA LINE.	
	10 "		Company relieved by the 55th M.G.Coy. 2 guns left in GRANDCOURT, remainder withdrawn. Half company proceeded to MARTINSART, half company remaining in THIEPVAL.	
	11 "			
	12 "		Half company in MARTINSART return to THIEPVAL.	

WAR DIARY
or
INTELLIGENCE SUMMARY.
(Erase heading not required.)

Army Form C. 2118.

Place	Date 1916	Hour	Summary of Events and Information	Remarks and references to Appendices
	13/11/16.		Relieved the 190th M.G. Coy. in section N of the ANCRE. 8 guns in BEAUCOURT Trench and 2 guns in reserve in old German First Line.	
	15/11 "		Relieved 3 guns of the 190th M.G. Coy. 2 guns in RIVER Trench and 1 gun in MIRAUMONT ALLEY.	
	16/11 "		Brigade attacked on SUNKEN ROAD from L.32.d.8.1. to MIRAUMONT ALLEY. 2 guns assembled in rear of 2nd wave of left company 1st R.M., 1 in rear of 2nd wave of Right company 1st R.M. and 1 in rear of 2nd R.M. to protect N. flank. P.O. Mallett with one gun; crew assembled at 2nd R.M. H.Q. and was to proceed to place of assembly prior to attack. Lieut. Barclay and 4 guns crew proceeded to RIVER TRENCH to take up positions. This section came under a barrage and suffered heavily, one gun being buried.	
	17/11 "	5.45 am	Barrage opened and attack started. 18th + 2nd Divisions attacked simultaneously on the right. 8 guns put up a barrage in front of SUNKEN ROAD while 12 guns of the 190th M.G. Coy put up a barrage on the N. and N.N.E. fronts. The gun on the left flank took up position at about R.2.b.1.7. The attack was successful, all objectives being gained. 1 gun took up position at about R.3.a.10.55. firing N.E. A captured German gun was mounted to fire E. One gun was located on the N. flank but owing to heavy casualties no ammunition was available.	
		4.30pm	R.5. position under Lieut. Wilkie, in RIVER TRENCH was demolished. The entrance to the dug out was blown out and the occupants had to be assisted out. All ammunition exploded and everything buried, excepting the gun which was withdrawn early in the morning of the 18th.	
	9/11 "		Relieved 3 guns of the 189th M.G. Coy. 1 in BAILLESCOURT FARM and 2 in SUNKEN ROAD. 1 O.R. wounded who remained at duty.	

Army Form C. 2118.

WAR DIARY
INTELLIGENCE SUMMARY.
(Erase heading not required.)

Instructions regarding War Diaries and Intelligence Summaries are contained in F. S. Regs. Part II. and the Staff Manual respectively. Title pages will be prepared in manuscript.

Place	Date 1917.	Hour	Summary of Events and Information	Remarks and references to Appendices
	18. Feb.	11.15 am	Enemy counter attacked in force from WUNDT WORK on N and N.E. front. Attack caught in our Barrage and repulsed with heavy loss, having failed to reach our lines.	
	19 "	2.25 am	S.O.S. received from the E. front. The enemy attack did not develop. S.O.S. cancelled 2.0. am. 8 guns of the 190th M.G. Coy were withdrawn from BEAUCOURT TRENCH and the remaining 8 placed under the Command of the O.C. 188th M.G. Coy. 1 gun under P.O.Staff took up position at the return N. of the SUNKEN ROAD.	
	20/21 "			
	21/22 "		2 guns of the 190th M.G. Coy were withdrawn from the N. flank, and 2 guns from BEAUCOURT TRENCH. German guns withdrawn from SUNKEN ROAD.	
	22 "		Half Company proceeded to MARTINSART.	
	22/23 "	2.30 pm	Relieved by 189th M.G. Coy. 8 guns being in front line, 4 in BEAUCOURT TRENCH and 4 in reserve. Remainder of Company proceeded to MARTINSART.	
	23 "			
	24 "			
	25 "	7.45 am	Arrived old German Front line.	
	27 "	11.0 pm	Returned to Martinsart.	
	28 "		at MARTINSART.	

W M McGeorge
2. Capt. H.L.I.
Acting O.C.
188th M.G. Coy.

APPENDIX "A".

ACTION BY 188th. and 190th. MACHINE GUN COMPANIES.

190th. M.G.Company. 1. 12 guns of the 190th. Machine Gun Company will be employed, under instructions issued by the Corps Machine Gun Officer, to place a barrage round the Northern and North Eastern flanks of the advance, from positions in the vicinity of GRANDCOURT and PUISIEUX ROAD.

The remaining four guns will be maintained in their present positions in R.2.a., and will be used for the defence of the present Northern flank held by the Brigade.

188th. M.G.Company 2. (a) 8 guns of the 188th. M.G.Company will be employed under instructions from Corps Machine Gun Officer, to bring a barrage fire on to the Eastern front of the objective from the vicinity of PUISIEUX ROAD, and OLD POST LINE.

The remaining 8 guns will be used as under :-

3 guns will take over the positions now held by guns of 190th. Machine Gun Company at R.2.b.05.4., R.2.b.3.0., and R.3.c.0.05., and will remain in these positions in defence, or for repelling counter-attacks.

(b) 2 guns will advance in rear of second wave of Left Company of 1st ROYAL MARINES and occupy positions in the vicinity of L.32.d.8.1., and R.2.i.9.9., the former position to enfilade the SUNKEN ROAD to the North, the latter to fire East and North-East.

(c) The 6th gun will move up with the second Company of HAWKE Battalion (reference para.9 of Brigade Order No.82.), and take up a position in the vicinity of R.2.b.3.7.

(d) The 7th gun will advance in rear of the second wave of the 1st ROYAL MARINES and take up a position at Point R.3.a.3.7., which is being consolidated as a Strong Point. This gun will be accomodated until ZERO hour beside the gun at R.2.b.05.4.

(e) The remaining gun will be accomodated until ZERO hour beside the gun now at R.2.b.3.0., and will advance in rear of the second wave of the Left Company of the HOWE Battalion and take up a position just East of SUNKEN ROAD in vicinity of R.3.a.2.5.

These guns, enumerated in sub-paras. (b),(c),(d), and (e), will cover the consolidation of the Northern and Eastern flanks.

3. A party of 10 men has been detailed by Officer Commanding HOWE Battalion as carrying party for the 5 guns taking part in the advance.

Captain.
Brigade Major.
188th. Infantry Brigade.

15th. February, 1917.

Army Form C. 2118.
Volume IX
188th Machine Gun Coy.

Vol XI

WAR DIARY
or
INTELLIGENCE SUMMARY.
(Erase heading not required.)

Place	Date 1917.	Hour	Summary of Events and Information	Remarks and references to Appendices
MARTINSART, BOUZINCOURT	2/18		Company moved from MARTINSART and Transport from ENGLEBELMER to BOUZINCOURT	
			Two guns attached to 17th Division. Other two at PUCHEVILLERS.	
do	5/19		Working parties were supplied for work on the roads	
do	19	9.30 am	Company moved to RUBEMPRE. Two guns on aerial guard at CONTAY rejoined unit.	
	20	8.55 am	Company moved to GEZAINCOURT. Two guns on aerial guard at PUCHEVILLERS rejoined unit.	
	21	10.32 am	Company moved to REBREUVE.	
	22	9.35 am	Company moved to BAUCHIN.	
	24	10.57 am	Company moved to SACHIN.	
	25	8.37 am	Company moved to ST HILAIRE.	
	26	9.10 am	Company moved to CALONNE-SUR-LA-LYS.	
	27	9. am	Company moved to NOEUX-LES-MINES.	
NOEUX-LES-MINES.	29/31.		Company training.	

W.M. Macgregor
1. Capt. H.L.I.
O.C.

186. Machine Gun Coy

Army Form C. 2118.

Volume X

WAR DIARY
INTELLIGENCE SUMMARY.
(Erase heading not required.)

Instructions regarding War Diaries and Intelligence Summaries are contained in F.S. Regs., Part II. and the Staff Manual respectively. Title pages will be prepared in manuscript.

Place	Date 1917	Hour	Summary of Events and Information	Remarks and references to Appendices
NOEUX-LES-MINES	1. April 10		Company training.	
	11. April		Company moved to DIEVAL.	
	11. Apr. 11.15 am		Company moved to DIEVAL.	
	12 "		at DIEVAL.	
	13 "			
	14 " 9.0 am		Company moved to ECOIVRES.	
	15 April		at ECOIVRES.	
	20 Apl.		Company moved to MAROEUIL.	
	21 "		5 Nos. 9 under Lieut. Dashwood reconnoitred positions for indirect fire opposite GAVRELLE. 8 guns took up positions W. of GAVRELLE for indirect fire, remaining 8 guns move to Railway Cutting. Transport & Q.M. stores at ST CATHERINES.	
	22 "		8 guns support the attack of 189th & 190th Infantry Brigade on GAVRELLE. 188th Machine Gun Coy. took over the line. 4 guns of 189th and 4 guns of 190th attached. Guns 5 of Benetic and in GAVRELLE, 6 guns in FOXY trench. 4 in old German front and support line.	
	23 "		Heavy shelling around GAVRELLE. 2 guns put out of action by shrapnel.	
	25 "		4 guns attacked to 1st R.M. and 4 to 2nd R.M. for attack on trenches in C.19.C.9.d. 4 guns attacked to 2nd R.M. suffered heavily from shell fire and snipers and all 4 guns were lost. The 4 guns with 1st R.M. failed to reach their positions owing to a German bombing attack from starting point where Railway crosses old German front line. Captured and 2 guns established there.	
	26 "		4 guns W. and returned to FOXY trench.	
	27/28 "			
	29 "			
	31 "		4 guns in FOXY and FOXY trenches.	

W.M. Gregor Capt M.G.C.
188th Bdr

188th Brigade (Infantry only) relieved by 93rd Infantry Brigade

"CONFIDENTIAL"

HEADQUARTERS,
188 M.G. Coy
late 223rd MACHINE GUN COMPANY

June 1917.

Vol 13

WAR DIARY
of
223rd MACHINE GUN COMPANY

from
1st MAY 1917
to.
31st MAY 1917

VOLUME II

with Appendix I

[signature]
Captain.
O.C. 223rd Machine Gun Company.

To A.G's OFFICE
3rd ECHELON.

223rd Machine Gun Company

Army Form C. 2118.

WAR DIARY
or
INTELLIGENCE SUMMARY.
(Erase heading not required.)

Instructions regarding War Diaries and Intelligence Summaries are contained in F. S. Regs., Part II. and the Staff Manual respectively. Title pages will be prepared in manuscript.

Place	Date May 1917	Hour	Summary of Events and Information	Remarks and references to Appendices
OURTON PAS DE CALAIS	1st		In billets	J.K.
"	2nd	9 am	Sent party of 2 officers 2Lt J. COOKE and 2Lt W. FITZGERALD, and 21 O.R. to be attached to 188 Machine Gun Company as carrying party	J.K.
"	3rd	8 pm	Carrying party rejoined	J.K. J.K.
"	4th		Billets	J.K.
"	5th		Move to MAGNICOURT-EN-COMTÉ. billeted with 2nd Field Ambulance 63rd (R.N.) Division and 224 M.G. Company	J.K.
MAGNICOURT-EN-COMTÉ	6/7th		in Billets	J.K.
"	8th	8 am	moved to VILLERS-BRULIN.	J.K.
VILLERS BRULIN	9th	5 pm	Took over equipment of 189th Machine Gun Company 63rd (R.N.) Division complete to Divisional H.Q. Reported taking over complete to Divisional H.Q.	J.K. J.K.
"	10th		In billets at VILLERS BRULIN	J.K.
"	11th	7:30 am	Company moved off from VILLERS-BRULIN to join the 189th Infantry Brigade 63rd (Royal Naval) Division.	J.K.
"		5 pm	Company arrived in new position at G.4.b.5.9. near ROCLINCOURT, and is now definitely the Machine Gun Company for the 189th Inf. Brigade	Ref. FRANCE Sheet 51BN.W. Edit 6A. J.K.

223rd Machine Gun Company
Army Form C. 2118.

WAR DIARY
or
INTELLIGENCE SUMMARY.
(Erase heading not required.)

Place	Date MAY 1917	Hour	Summary of Events and Information	Remarks and references to Appendices
ROCLINCOURT	16th		In bivouacs at G.46.5.8. Ordinary machine gunners training was done during this period	Ref. FRANCE 51. S.W. 2a etc. J.K.
"	17th		Received copy of 189th Inf. Brigade Order No. 93 of 17/5/17 ref. to move of 63rd Division into the line on the night of the 20th May, to relieve the 31st Division. The 189th Infantry Brigade to go into divisional Reserve on that date with the machine gun company at ST CATHERINE.	J.K.
"	18th/19th		Training	J.K.
"	20th		10 O.R. joined the company 18/5/17 from M.G. Corps Base depot. Company moved to ST CATHERINE taking over Billets vacated by 92nd Machine Gun Company. Headquarters at the DISTILLERY. The transport lines remained in their present position at G.4.a.	J.K.
STE. CATHERINE	20th			
	23rd		During this period officers reconnoitred the sectors held by the 188th and 190th Infantry Brigades at GAVRELLE and OPPY respectively.	J.K.
	24th		Received copy of Reserve Brigade Defence Scheme for the GAVRELLE Sector.	J.K.
	25th/27th		Training	J.K.

223rd Machine Gun Company.
Army Form C. 2118.

WAR DIARY
or
INTELLIGENCE SUMMARY.
(Erase heading not required.)

Place	Date 1917	Hour	Summary of Events and Information	Remarks and references to Appendices
STE. CATHERINE	MAY 28th		Received copy of Warning Operation order B.M. 542 of 189th Infantry Brigade for an attack which was to be made on GAVRELLE and SOUTH GAVRELLE TRENCHES at a later date	X.
do	29th		Warning operation order B.M. 542 cancelled.	R.
do	30th		Received copy of 189th Infantry Brigade order No 94 of 30/5/17, containing orders for the relief of the 190th Infantry Brigade by the 189th Infantry Brigade in the left sector of the divisional front on the night 1/2 June. The 223rd Machine Gun Company to relieve the 190th Machine Gun Company on the night of the 2nd/3rd June.	
do	31st		The transport of the company was inspected by the G.O.C. 63rd (R.N) Division Major General LAWRIE, CB., D.S.O. Issued Relief order No.1 to all concerned	R. see Appendix No 1. B.

SECRET.   WAR DIARY   COPY No. 1

RELIEF ORDER NO. 1
by
CAPTAIN J. B. DODGE, D. S. C.
Commanding 223rd. Machine Gun Company.

30th. May, 1917.

Ref. Map - 51B N.W. 1/20,000.

1. The 189th. Infantry Brigade will relieve the 190th. Infantry Brigade in the left sector of divisional front on the night of June 1/2nd.
    The 223rd. Machine Gun Company will relieve the 190th. Machine Gun Company on the night of June 2/3rd.

2. Relief of sections and gunteams of 190th. M. G. Coy. will be carried out in accordance with the attached Table of Relief.

3. Location of Units on completion of Relief :-
  (a). Brigade Headquarters - B.21 a 7.7.
  (b). Right front line battalion - Hood Bn. - c 11 c 90.05 to B.24 b 2.1.
      Battalion H.Q. at B. 30 a 8.9.
  (c). Left front line battalion - Hawke Bn. - B.18.a.9.2. to B.24.b.2.1.
      Battalion H.Q. at B.17.c.6.2.
  (d). Support Battalion - Nelson Bn. -
    3 Coys. in Railway Cutting in B.21.c.
    1 Coy. in Trench at B.17.c.
      Battalion H.Q. at B.21.c.8.7.
  (e). Reserve Battalion - Drake Bn. - in trench system B.25.d.
      Battalion H.Q. at B.25.d.9.6.
  (f). 223rd. M. G. Coy. H.Q. at B.28.a.5.8.

4. All trench stores, aeroplane photographs, Defence Schemes and all other documents concerning the line will be taken over by incoming Section Officers from the officers whom they relieve. Receipts for these will be forwarded to Coy. H.Q. by 4 a.m. runner on 3rd. June.

5. Box respirators will be worn in the alert position during the relief. A gas sentry will be placed at the entrance to each dug-out.

6. Great coats will be taken into the line, but not packs.

7. The attention of all officers is drawn to notes on Trench Standing Orders, and to list of Returns which have been circulated to them.

8. M. G. Coy. Headquarters of Sections :-
  Southern Defence - Section H.Q.   B.24.d.05.50.
  Red Line   -   do.   B.16.b.3.1.
  Northern Defence -   do.   B.17.c.60.30.
  Reserve Sector   H   do.   B.28.a.5.8.

9. RATIONS. Rations will be made up by gunteams, and also separately for Section Headquarters. The ration return due at 5-0 a.m. daily will give number of men to each gunteam, or Section H.Q. The Q.M.S. will see that the Ration Bags are made up and marked according to this return. The bags will be dumped by the Transport at Maison de la Cote nightly at 8-0 p.m. The Reserve Section will carry the rations from that point to Coy. H.Q. Ration parties from each gunteam in the line will assemble at Coy. H.Q. at 9-0 p.m. and take up rations and water when they arrive. Attention is particularly drawn to the necessity for returning all empty petrol tins to Coy. H.Q. by Ration Party. Unless an empty tin is received a full one cannot be given in exchange.

10. STRENGTH OF GUNTEAMS. No gunteam in the line will consist of more than one N.C.O. and four men. All spare numbers will be left behind in the Transport Lines. Nominal Rolls will be handed in to Orderly Room by 9-0 a.m. 1/6/17, shewing -
   (a). Nominal Roll and number of each gunteam in trench.
   (b). Nominal Roll of personnel left behind.

11. The following stores will be taken by Nos. 1, 2 & 3 Sections when they relieve,
   (a). Guns and spare barrels. (b). Spare parts boxes and first aid cases. (c). Cleaning rods. (d). Condensers and tubes.
   Number 4 Section will take in complete gun equipment. Nos. 1, 2 & 3 Sections will take over from the Sections they relieve - (a). Belt boxes. (b). Tripods.
   Guns will be carried in trench cases.

12. Packs of men going into the line, will be dumped at Q.M.S. Stores by 2-0 p.m. 2/6/17. They will be properly marked at the bottom with the Regimental Number and Name of owned.

13. Detail of Relief. The leading Section on arrival at B.26.c.3.3. will halt and take gun gear, rations, &c, from the limbers. Guides from 190th. Company will be at this point at 8-30 p.m. and will conduct them to the Brown line. Each Section in moving up the Brown Line will keep an interval of 50 yards between teams, and 100 yards interval between Sections. When halted this interval should remain the same.

14. Section Officers will be most careful to check and give receipts for (a). All trench stores handed over to them. (b). All gun equipment handed over to them. These receipts will be forwarded to Coy. H.Q. as early as possible.

15. The Transport Officer will arrange to hand over to 190 M.G. Coy. in exchange gun equipment enumerated on these receipts.

16. Signallers. Three Signallers under Corporal Goode will report to 190 M.G. Coy. H.Q. at 2-0 p.m. on the 2/6/17 and ascertain the working signalling arrangements. He will arrange before darkness to relieve the instrument of 190 M.G. Coy. and instal his own.

17. Advance party. An advance party of One Officer, One Sgt. and Four Nos. 2 per Section will go to 190 M.G. H.Q. with their Transport Ration Party on 1/6/17. They will be attached to Gunteams in the line for the night of the 1/2nd June, and will gain all possible information regaring their positions, orders for same, &c. Time of move will be notified later.

_____ ADJUTANT

223 MACHINE GUN COY. M.G.C.

RELIEF TIME TABLE.

SECTION.	OFFICERS IN CHARGE.	SECTOR TO BE RELIEVED.	NO. OF GUNS.	GUN POSITIONS NOS.
No. 1	Lt. Waterson.	Southern front line sector.	4	1, 2, 3 & 4.
No. 2	2/Lt. Cooke.		2	5 & 6.
No. 2	2/Lt. McLaren.	Southern Support Guns.	2	7 & 8.
No. 3.	2/Lt. Sidwell.	Northern Support Gun & Red Line.	1 3	9 10, 11 & 12.
NO. 4.	2/Lt. Jones. 2/Lt. Fitzgerald. 2/Lt. Griffiths.	Reserve Section Coy. H.Q.	4	13, 14, 15 & 16

"CONFIDENTIAL"

Headquarters
188th Machine Gun Company
9th July 1917

Vol 14

WAR DIARY of
188TH MACHINE GUN COMPANY
(Late 223rd)

from
1st JUNE 1917
to
30th JUNE 1917.

VOLUME III. with Appendix No. 2.

J B Hodge Capt
O.C. 188th Machine Gun Company

To/ A.G's Office
3rd Echelon.

223rd Machine Gun Company
(New=188th)   Army Form C. 2118.

WAR DIARY
or
INTELLIGENCE SUMMARY.
(Erase heading not required.)

Place	Date 1917	Hour	Summary of Events and Information	Remarks and references to Appendices
SAINTE CATHERINE	JUNE 1st		Advance party of officers and men left to be attached to 190 Machine Gun Company in the line in the left sector of the divisional front with a view to becoming thoroughly acquainted with the situation before its relief of 190 M.G. Coy. The 189th Brigade less 223rd M.G. Coy. relieved the 190th Inf Bde. less 190 M.G. Coy. in the left sector of the divisional front.	J.F.
do	2nd		The Company relieved 190 M.G. Coy. in the line.	J.F.
TRENCHES	3rd	2.30 am	Relief of 190 M.G. Coy complete. Company Headquarters in Gun Pit at B.28.a.5.8. Brigade H.Q. being in the Railway Cutting at B.21.a.7.4. The dispositions of the Brigade were as follows. 2 Battalions Roca in the front line. One in support and one in Reserve. The dispositions of the Machine Gun Company were. 4 guns in the front line, 4 guns in support, 2 guns in the RED (Reserve) LINE and 4 guns in Reserve at Company H.Q.	Ref FRANCE 51.B NW 1/20,000
B.29.a.5.8	4th		The Brigade front was thoroughly reconnoitred, and as the gun were not placed so as to be of the best use in action, several gun positions were changed. 1 O.R. killed in action	M.

2,2,3rd Machine Gun Coy
(now 188th) Army Form C. 2118.

WAR DIARY
or
INTELLIGENCE SUMMARY.
(Erase heading not required.)

Place	Date 1917	Hour	Summary of Events and Information	Remarks and references to Appendices
TRENCHES B2a & 8.	June 5th		In accordance with a set plan the company took part in a programme of operations involving the cooperation of machine guns with the artillery. The heavy howitzers commenced cutting the enemy's wire and damaging his trenches and machine gun fire was employed to prevent him as far as possible from doing any work of repair on his wire or his trenches. A list of targets was drawn up. The machine guns also cooperated with the artillery in practical barrage, which was put up daily. The number of rounds fired was roughly 8000 per day.	JT
do	6/17		programmes of firing were carried out as on the 5th. 1 O.R. wounded in action.	A
do	7th	2pm	Received news that the 2nd Army had made an attack at 3.10 am between ZILLEBEKE and PLOEGSTEERT WOOD had taken MESSINES and first and second objectives	A
do	8th.		The machine guns of the company again cooperated with the artillery Barrages during the night of the 8th inst. Large raids were	

188th Machine Gun Company
Vol 223 Army Form C. 2118.

WAR DIARY
or
~~INTELLIGENCE SUMMARY.~~
(Erase heading not required.)

Place	Date	Hour	Summary of Events and Information	Remarks and references to Appendices
B.28a.5.8.	June 9th		Relief made by the XVII Corps on the night and by the CANADIAN CORPS on the left and cooperation by all arms of the XIII Corps was necessary in order to keep the enemy off also our post on the Qui-vive. Enemy tracks etc were swept and traversed by machine gun fire.	J2.
do	9th		Received copy of 189th Inf. Bde. Order No. 97, with reference to the relief of the 189th Brigade by the 94th Inf. Bde. on the night 10/11th June and 11/12th June respectively. Issued Relief order No. 2 to all concerned. See Appendix No. 2.	See Appendix No. 2
do	13th		Lt. S.F. WATERSON proceeded on a course to the Machine Gun School G.H.Q. Infantry battalions of the 189th S/Bde relieved by infantry battalions of the 94th Inf. Bde.	K.
do	14th	9pm	Relief of company by the 94th M.G. Coy.	J.
do	15th	2am	Relief complete. Company moved to billets in MAROEUIL and in accordance with orders received became the 188th Machine Gun Company and thenceforward came under the orders of the 188th Infantry Brigade. During the period in the line the company was fairly active	

188th Machine Gun Company
(late 223) Army Form C. 2118.

WAR DIARY
or
INTELLIGENCE SUMMARY.
(Erase heading not required.)

Place	Date	Hour	Summary of Events and Information	Remarks and references to Appendices
MAROEUIL	June 1917	p.m.	Many machine gun positions which on coming into the line were found to be unsuitable were changed and so far as possible the machine gun defences of the sector were rearranged so as to give belts of crossfire across the front and also to cooperate with the guns in the sectors both on the right and the left. Much attention to find direct fire was carried out, mostly in cooperation with the artillery. Contact was established with the headquarters of the nearest artillery Brigade and several useful target maps were obtained. Firing programmes were accordingly drawn up and were based on these target maps which included several varieties of trench targets. Special attention was also paid to enemy tracks and much help was derived from the study of the most recent aeroplane photographs. In picking out targets a daylight indirect fire shoot was also tried during this period but owing to unfavourable climatic conditions the artillery observer could not obtain any observation of the fire.	/k

186th Machine Gun Coy
Army Form C. 2118

WAR DIARY
or
INTELLIGENCE SUMMARY.
(Erase heading not required.)

Place	Date	Hour	Summary of Events and Information	Remarks and references to Appendices
MAROEUIL	June 13th 1917		A training programme was drawn out and training commenced. The hours of training allotted were from 7.0 am to 10.30 am daily. The first weeks training to include infantry training and visual training, the second week elementary machine gun training including the firing of Pt I of the Vickers Machine Gun course and Revolver Course and the third week advanced machine gun work, including section and company tactical schemes and machine gun course and the firing of Pt II of the general machine gun course. The 62nd division was now in Corps Reserve. The following letter was received from the XIII Corps Commander by the G.O.C. 63rd (R.N.) Division after the division had been relieved. "From inspection of the trenches and examination of photographs I gather that your division has dug in its capture of the trenches as well as it fought in its capture of GAVRELLE. Please convey to all ranks my satisfaction and thanks. (Sd) W.M. Congreve Lieut General.	

188th Machine Gun Company.
Army Form C. 2118.

WAR DIARY
or
INTELLIGENCE SUMMARY.
(Erase heading not required.)

Instructions regarding War Diaries and Intelligence Summaries are contained in F.S. Regs., Part II. and the Staff Manual respectively. Title pages will be prepared in manuscript.

Place	Date 1917	Hour	Summary of Events and Information	Remarks and references to Appendices
MAROEUIL	June 18th		Training	IL
do	19th		The 188th Infantry Brigade was inspected by Admiral Lord Charles BERESFORD and the 1st Army Commander General Sir W. HORNE K.C.B.	JL
do	20/22		Training	IL
do	23rd		Company Sports held	IL
do	24th		Unsuccessful	IL
do	25th		The Company was inspected by the Crown PRINCE of SIAM. The organisation of a machine gun company was explained to him, and a short exercise including action from limbers and opening fire quickly on a target was carried out.	IL
do	26th-28th		Uneventful	IL
do	29th		Lt. S.F. WATERSON rejoined from course at M.G. School CAMIERS.	IL
do	30th		2/Lt E.H. JONES left for course at G.HQ Small Arms School CAMIERS.	IL

T2134. Wt. W708—776. 500000. 4/15. Sir J. C. & S.

SECRET.

"WAR DIARY."

APPENDIX No 2.

RELIEF ORDER NO 2
By
Captain J.B. Dodge, D.S.O.,
Commanding 223 Machine Gun Company.

1. The 223rd Machine Gun Company will be relieved by the 94th Machine Gun Company on the night of the 11/12th insts.

2. On completion of relief the Company will be located at Maroeuil.

3. All trench stores, aeroplane photographs, documents, and maps giving dispositions and work being done in the sectors commanded by Section Officers will be handed over to relieving Sections and receipts obtained. The following will be the procedure for this handing over of trench stores :-
   (a) Each Section Officer will make out in triplicate a list of trench stores for each gun position. He will give these lists to the N.C.O. i/c position, who will have these lists signed by the relieving N.C.O. He will give one copy to the relieving N.C.O., and return the other two copies to his Section Officer, who will hand them in to Company H.Q.
   (b) With regard to Trench Maps only, these will be handed over direct by Section Officers, & a receipt obtained from the relieving Officer.

4. Gas Helmets will be worn in the "Alert" position during the relief.

5. Transport Officer will arrange to take over the billets at present occupied by the 94th Machine Gun Company at Maroeuil. The Transport lines of the 223rd Machine Gun Company will remain in their present location. Q.M. Stores will move to Maroeuil on the morning of the 11th inst.
   Tea will be provided for each Section on arrival at billets. C.Q.M.S. will make arrangements for this.

6. RELIEF.
   (a) Guides. One guide each from Nos 1, 2, 3, 4, 5, 6, 7, 8, 9, 10, 11, & 12 gun positions will report at Company H.Q. at 5.30 a.m. on Monday 11th inst. Each guide should bring his day's rations with him, & have his water bottle filled. He will remain at Company H.Q. during the day, & after dusk will go to meet the relieving Company at B.25d9.1, whence he will guide his relief direct to its gun position.
   (b) The reserve Section at Company H.Q. will be relieved by guns. Guides will be sent from Company H.Q. as in para (a)
   NOTE 1. Section Officers will ensure that the guides they send are absolutely trustworthy, & know the way thoroughly. The Section Officer's runner should be sent in the cases of 2/Lts Griffiths & Sidwell as one of the guides.
   NOTE 2. Section Officers will take steps to give each guide a slip of paper shewing the number of the gun position for which he is guide.

7. At all gun positions belt boxes will be handed over to the relieving gun teams.
   All other gun equipment, i.e., guns, tripods, trench bags, condensers, spare parts, cleaning rods, spare barrels, very pistols, etc., will be brought out.

8. REPORTING. As soon as teams are relieved, they will come back independently to Company H.Q., where they will wait until the Section Officer arrives and reports Relief Complete to the O.C. Company. Section Officers will then march their Sections to the limbers, which will be in waiting on the ARRAS - BAILLEUL Road at B.26.c.3.3., load up the guns, &c., and march back independently to Billets.

RELIEF ORDER NO. 2. (Cont'd.)

9. **LIMBERS.** The Transport Officer will arrange to have 4 limbers (one per Section) at B.26.c.3.3. at 11-0 p.m. on the 11th. inst. These limbers will then await the arrival of their Sections, and will transport gun gear to Maroeuil.

10. Section Officers will instruct their N. C. O's to check the Arms and Equipment of the men, and report any deficiencies when the Company is back in Rest Billets.

.... Lt. & Adjt.
223rd. Machine Gun Company.

June 9th. 1917.

"Confidential."

Headquarters
188th Machine Gun Company
1st July 1917

Vol 14

War of Diary
188th Machine Gun Company
(late 223rd)

from 1st June 1917
to 30th June 1917.

Volume III with Appendix No 2.

J.R. Bridge Capt
O.C. 188th Machine Gun Company

To/ O/c
A.G's Office
Base

188th Machine Gun Company
(late 223rd)

Army Form C. 2118.

WAR DIARY
or
INTELLIGENCE SUMMARY.
(Erase heading not required.)

Place	Date 1917	Hour	Summary of Events and Information	Remarks and references to Appendices
SAINTE CATHERINE	June 1st		Advance party of officers and men left to be attached to 190 Machine Gun Company in the line in the left sector of the divisional front with a view to becoming thoroughly acquainted with the situation before the relief of 190 M.G. Coy. the 189th Brigade less 223rd M.G.Coy relieved the 190th Inf Bde, less 190 M.G.Coy in the left sector of the divisional front	
do	2nd		The company relieved 190 M.G. Coy. in the line	9b
do	3rd	2.30am	Relief of 190 M.G. Coy complete. Company headquarters in gunpit at B28a5.8. Brigade H.Q. being in the Railway Cutting at B21a7.9. The dispositions of the Brigade were as follows:- 2 Battalions holding the front line, one in support and one in reserve. The dispositions of the machine gun company were as follows:- 6 guns in the front line, 4 guns in support, 2 guns in the RED (Reserve) LINE and 4 guns in reserve at Company HQ.	Ref FRANCE Sheet 51 B NW 1/10,000
TRENCHES B28a5.8.	4th		The Brigade front was thoroughly reconnoitred and, as the guns were not placed so as to be of the best use in action, several gun positions were changed. 1.O.R. killed in action	9L
do	5th		In accordance with a set plan, the company took part in a programme of	9L

188th Machine Gun Company.
(late 223rd)

Army Form C. 2118.

WAR DIARY
or
INTELLIGENCE SUMMARY.
(Erase heading not required.)

Place	Date	Hour	Summary of Events and Information	Remarks and references to Appendices
TRENCHES B28 a 5.8	June 5th		of operations involving the cooperation of the machine guns with the artillery. The heavy howitzers commenced cutting the enemy's wire and damaging his trenches and machine gun fire was employed to prevent him as far as possible from doing any work of repair on his wire or his trenches. A list of targets was drawn up. The machine guns also cooperated with the artillery in practice barrages which were put up daily. The number of rounds fired was roughly 8000 per day.	Y.
do	6/7th		Programmes of firing were carried out as on the 5th. 1O.R. wounded in action	Y.
do	7th	3 pm	Received news that the 2nd Army had made an attack at 3.10 am between ZILLEBEKE and PLOEGSTEERT WOOD, had taken MESSINES and their 1st and 2nd objectives.	Y.
do	8th		The machine guns of the company again cooperated with the artillery Barrages during the night of the 8th inst. Large raids were being made by the XVII Corps on the right and by the CANADIAN CORPS on the left and cooperation by all arms of the XIII Corps was necessary in order to keep the enemy opposite our front on the qui-vive. Enemy tracks etc were swept and traversed by machine gun fire.	Y.

188th Machine Gun Company (late 223rd)

Army Form C. 2118.

WAR DIARY
INTELLIGENCE SUMMARY.
(Erase heading not required.)

Place	Date 1917 June	Hour	Summary of Events and Information	Remarks and references to Appendices
TRENCHES B28 a 5 8	9th		Received copy of 189th Inf. Bde. Order No. 97 with reference to the relief of the 189th Inf. Brigade by the 94th Inf. Bde. on the night 10/11th June and 11/12th June respectively. Issued Relief order No. 2 to all concerned.	See Appendix No. 2.
do	10th		LT. S.F. WATERSON proceeded on a course to the Machine Gun School G.H.Q. Infantry battalions of the 189th Inf. Bde. relieved by infantry Battalions of the 94th Inf. Bde.	do
do	11th	9.0 pm	Relief of company by the 94th M.G. Coy.	do
do	12th	2.0 am	Relief complete. Company moved to billets in MAROEUIL and in accordance with orders	
MAROEUIL			received, became the 188th Machine Gun Company and thenceforward came under the orders of the 188th Infantry Brigade. During the period in the line the Company was fairly active. Many machine gun positions, which, on coming into the line were found to be unsuitable, were changed, and, as far as possible the machine gun defences of the sector were so rearranged as to give belts of crossfire across the front and also to cooperate with the guns in the sectors both on the right and on the left. With regard to firing, much indirect fire was carried out, mostly in cooperation with the artillery. Contact was established with the headquarters of the nearest artillery brigade and several useful target maps were obtained	

188th Machine Gun Company
(late 223rd)

Army Form C. 2118.

WAR DIARY
or
INTELLIGENCE SUMMARY.

(Erase heading not required.)

Place	Date	Hour	Summary of Events and Information	Remarks and references to Appendices
MAROEUIL	June 1917 12th		firing programmes were accordingly drawn up and were based on these target maps which included every variety of trench target. Special attention was also paid to enemy tracks and much help was derived from the study of the most recent aeroplane photographs in picking out targets. A daylight indirect fire shoot was also tried during this period but owing to unfavourable climatic conditions the artillery observer could not obtain any observation of the fire.	1/2
do	13th		A training programme was drawn out and training commenced. The hours of training allotted were from 7.0 a.m. to 10.30 a.m. daily. The first week's training to include infantry training and manual training, the second week elementary machine gun training including the firing of Pt I General machine gun course and Revolver course: the third week advanced machine gun work and the firing of Part II General machine gun course. The 63rd division was now in Corps Reserve. The following letter was received from the XIII Corps Commander by the G.O.C. 63rd (R.N.) Division, after the division had been relieved "from inspection of the trenches	

188th Machine Gun Company
(late 223rd)

Army Form C. 2118.

WAR DIARY
INTELLIGENCE SUMMARY.
(Erase heading not required.)

Place	Date 1917	Hour	Summary of Events and Information	Remarks and references to Appendices
MARŒUIL	June 13th		and examination of photographs. I gather that your division has dug during its late tour of the trenches as well as it fought in its capture of GAVRELLE. Please convey to all ranks my satisfaction and thanks – (Sd) W.H. Congreve Lieutenant General.	A
do	14/15/16/17/18/19th		Training	do
do			The 188th Infantry Brigade was inspected by Admiral Lord CHARLES BERESFORD and the 1st Army Commander, General Sir W. HORNE, K.C.B.	B
do	20/21/22/23/24/25th		Training	do
do			The company was inspected by the CROWN PRINCE of SIAM. The organisation of a machine gun company was explained to him and a short exercise, including action from limbers and opening fire quickly on a target, was carried out.	C
do	26/27/28th		uneventful	D
do	29th		Lieut. S.F. WATERSON rejoined from Course at M.G. School CAMIERS	E
do	30th		Lieut E.A. JONES left for course at G.H.Q. Small Arms School CAMIERS	F

SECRET.   RELIEF ORDER NO. 2   WAR DIARY
                            by
~~5. Company.~~   Captain J. B. Dodge, D.S.C.   Appendix No 2
                    Commanding 223 Machine Gun Company.

1.   The 223rd. Machine Gun Company will be relieved by the
    94th. Machine Gun Company on the night of the 11th./12th. insts.

2.   On completion of relief the Company will be located at
    Maroeuil.

3.   All trench stores, aeroplane photographs, documents, and
    maps giving dispositions and work being done in the sectors
    commanded by Section Officers will be handed over to relieving
    Sections and receipts obtained. The following will be the
    procedure for this handing over of trench stores :-
    (a).   Each Section Officer will make out in triplicate a
            list of trench stores for each gunteam position. He will
            give these lists to the N. C. O. i/c position, who will
            have them signed by the relieving N. C. O. He will give
            one copy to the relieving N. C. O., and return the other
            two copies to his Section Officer, who will hand them in to
            Company H. Q.
    (b).   With regard to <u>Trench Maps only</u>, these will be handed
            direct by Section Officers, and a receipt obtained from the
            relieving Officer.

4.   Gas Helmets will be worn in the "Alert" position during
    the relief.

5.   Transport Officer will arrange to take over the Billets at
    present occupied by the 94th. Machine Gun Company at Maroeuil.
    The Transport lines of the 223rd. Machine Gun Company will remain
    in their present location. Q.M. Stores will move to Maroeuil
    on the morning of the 11th. inst.
        Tea will be provided for each Section on arrival at Billets.
    C.Q.M.S. will make arrangements for this.

6. <u>RELIEF</u>.
    (a).   <u>Guides</u>. One guide from each of Nos. 1,2,3,4,5,6,7,8,9,
            10,11 & 12 gun positions will report at Company H.Q. at
            8-30 a.m. on Monday, 11th. inst. Each guide <u>should bring
            his day's rations with him, and have his water bottle
            filled.</u> He will remain at Company H. Q. during the day,
            and after dusk will go to meet the relieving Company at
            B.25.d.9.1., whence he will guide his relief to it's
            gun position.
    (b).   The reserve Section at Company H.Q. will be relieved
            by guns. Guides will be sent from Company H.Q. as in
            para. (a).
    <u>NOTE 1</u>. Section Officers will insure that the guides they send
            are <u>absolutely trustworthy</u>, and know the way thoroughly.
            The Section Officer's runner should be sent in the cases of
            2/Lts. Griffiths and Sidwell as one of the guides.
    <u>NOTE 2</u>. Section Officers will take steps to give each guide
            a slip of paper shewing the number of the gun position for
            which he is guide.

7.   At all gun positions belt boxes will be handed over to
    the relieving gun teams.
        All other gun equipment, i.e., guns, tripods, trench bags,
    condensers, spare parts, cleaning rods, spare barrels, very
    pistols, &c, will be brought out.

8. <u>REPORTING</u>.   As soon as teams are relieved, they will come back
    independedly to Company H. Q., where they will wait until the
    Section Officer arrives and reports Relief Complete to the O. C.
    Company. Section Officers will then march their Sections to the
    limbers which will be in waiting on the ARRAS - BAILLEUL Road
    at B.26.c.3.3., load up the guns, &c., and march back
    independently to Billets.

RELIEF ORDER NO. 2. (Cont'd.)

9. **LIMBERS.** The Transport Officer will arrange to have 4 limbers (one per Section) at B.26.c.3.3. at 11-0 p.m. on the 11th. inst. These limbers will then await the arrival of their Sections, and will transport gun gear to Maroeuil.

10. Section Officers will instruct their N.C.O's to check the Arms and Equipment of the men, and report any deficiencies when the Company is back in Rest Billets.

.... Lt. & Adjt.
223rd. Machine Gun Company.

June 9th. 1917.

Issued to all concerned

CONFIDENTIAL.

Headquarters.
188th. Machine Gun Company

Vol 1 Aug 1st 1917.

WAR DIARY
of
188th Machine Gun Company

from
1st July 1917.
to
31st July. 1917.

VOLUME No. A with Appendices Nos. 3, 4, 5, 6, 7 & 8

J B Singer Capt.
Commanding 188th Machine Gun Company.

To/ A.G's Office
3rd Echelon

63a

Subject:- Duplicate War Diaries.

To:- OC

188th M.G. Coy

C.R. No. 8700/1054

The enclosed Duplicate War Diary is returned to you please, as "Duplicates" are not required in this Office, vide:- General Routine Order, No. 1125. 1698

To Home Records London

J.C.Yale?

General Headquarters,
3rd Echelon,
23/9/1916

Staff-Captain, DAAG
for D.A.G.

188 Machine Gun Company.

To D.A.G. Base.

Re WAR DIARY.

This is not a duplicate WAR DIARY but the *original*.

The colour of the pencil has apparently led to the mistake.

.... Lieut & Adj

For Captain Commanding 188 Machine Gun Company.

To / Secret
A.G. Office
3rd Echelon

25/8/17

Herewith War
Diary for July
which has been
returned to us
by the Machine Gun
Corps Section of the
A.G. Office

E Hugh Jones
2/Lt A/Adjt
188 M.G. Coy

188th Machine Gun Company
Army Form C. 2118.

WAR DIARY
or
INTELLIGENCE SUMMARY.
(Erase heading not required.)

Place	Date 1917	Hour	Summary of Events and Information	Remarks and references to Appendices
MAROEUIL	JULY 1st		Uneventful. Lt W. FITZGERALD proceeded on leave to U.K.	K.
do	2nd		Received Copies of 188th Infantry Brigade Orders No 119 and 120 containing instructions for the relief of the Battalions of the 93rd Infantry Brigade 31st Division holding the right sector of the divisional front in front of GAVRELLE village on the night 3/4th July and for the relief of the 93rd Machine Gun Company by the 188th Machine Gun Company on the night 4/5th June. Reconnaissance of June by officer. Company moved to billets in STE CATHERINE St.	
STE.CATHERINE	3rd 4th			
	5.	3am	Relief of 93rd Machine Gun Company completed. Dispositions of guns see Appendix No 3. Headquarters in dugouts at H.1.c.Y.4. Advanced Company H.Q. at B.28.c.4.2. Y. The guns of the company were disposed as follows:- (a) FRONT LINE GROUP 4 guns (No 4 Section) (b) SUPPORT LINE GROUP 4 guns (No 1 Sect) (c) (4.1 No 2 and 2 of No 3) RED LINE GROUP 2 guns (No 3 Sect) 6 guns here in Reserve at rear Coy. H.Q. at H.1.c.7.4. in charge of each group. 6 guns of front line guns were as follows Covering and battle lines (No 1) gun C.25.d.20. T.B. 135° (No 2) C.25.c.93. T.B. 120° (No 3) C.25.c.48. T.B. 15° (No 4) C.25.a.65.60. T.B. 150°	APPENDIX No 3. Ref. Map FRANCE 51B N.W 1/20,000

WAR DIARY

INTELLIGENCE SUMMARY
(Erase heading not required.)

Army Form C. 2118.

128th Machine Gun Company

Instructions regarding War Diaries and Intelligence Summaries are contained in F.S. Regs., Part II. and the Staff Manual respectively. Title pages will be prepared in manuscript.

Place	Date	Hour	Summary of Events and Information	Remarks and references to Appendices
TRENCHES Coy H.Q. at H6c7.4.5.	5th		Support line guns (No 5.) gun H6a4.5. T.B.45° (No 6) gun H6a 5.8 T.A.45° (No 7) gun B30a 30.45 T.B. 116° (No 8) gun B30 a 60.65 T.B. 60°. Red line guns No 9 gun H5a 8.4. T.B. 110°; No 10 gun T4b80.90. T.B. 60°. Communication between Company H.Q. and the guns in the line was established by means of relay posts of runners and telephone. Relay posts were situated at Advanced Company H.Q. at B28c4.2 and the H.Q. of the Officer I/c Support line guns at H6a 5.8. Coy H.Q. was in telephonic communication with the Brigade H.Q. at BOIS DE LA MAISON BLANCHE and with Advanced Company H.Q. at B28 c4.2. The relay system of runners was found to work very well and it involved few lining journeys for runners.	Ref: France Sheet 51B N.W. 1/20,000 Trench Map
	6th		Uneventful.	X.
	7th		Uneventful.	X.
	8th		Arrangements were made by the divisional M.G. Officer for 2 more guns to be put into position in the RED LINE at B29a15.80 (No 14 gun) J. Bearing arc of fire 145° and at B29a1.7. No 15 gun T.B. arc of fire 51°.	X.

188th Machine Gun Company.
Army Form C. 2118.

WAR DIARY
or
INTELLIGENCE SUMMARY.
(Erase heading not required.)

Place	Date July	Hour	Summary of Events and Information	Remarks and references to Appendices
TRENCHES	8th.		These guns were taken from the reserve guns at Coy H.Q. They occupied anti aircraft positions by day and were mounted in their Battle emplacements by night.	9k.
do	9th.		Lieut S.F. WATERSON evacuated to No 30 Casualty Clearing Station	9k.
do	10th.		Inter section relief. New B.A.D. French Code No 3 came into use to replace the old Code 15. No 2. No 1 Section now holding the front line group No 3 the Suffolk line group and No 2 the Red line group	see Appendix No. 4. 9k.
do	11th.		As the dispositions of the guns in the line was not found to be satisfactory they were altered to new positions by arrangement with the divisional M.G. officer and the G.O.C. 188th Inf Bde. A new system of numbering the guns was also introduced so that guns worked of being numbered by Brigade sectors were to be numbered consecutively along the divisional front. The new numbers and positions of the guns were as follows. Front line group. No 1 gun I 1 b 00.95 T.B. 345°; No 4 gun C 25 c 10. 25. T.B. 133° No 5 gun C 25 c 15.30 T.B. 26° No 13 gun B 30 d 5.2 T.B. 3°	

WAR DIARY
INTELLIGENCE SUMMARY
(Erase heading not required.)

188th Machine Gun Company

Army Form C. 2118.

Place	Date	Hour	Summary of Events and Information	Remarks and references to Appendices
TRENCHES	July 11th		Support line guns. No 14 gun H6a 55. T.B. 45°: No 15 gun H6a 5.9. T.B. 25° No 16 gun B30c 4.4. T.B. 30° No 17 gun B24 A2.1. T.B. 28°. The RED LINE guns remained as before. Emplacements were dug for these new positions and also Range Cards prepared. Alternative positions were also sited and prepared for each gun and special ammunition Box mountings were fitted into the parapet of the trench at the places selected. These mountings did not necessitate the use of the MK IV tripod as they only required the crosshead and socket of the Tripod. The mounting was built into the parapet and it had a slot to received the socket of the tripod. These emplacements were also much less conspicuous than the positions ordinarily prepared to receive the MK IV Tripod. A good deal of work was done in making recesses for ammunition belt boxes at the new positions and generally improving the positions.	J.R.
	12th/13th		uneventful. uneventful.	

188th Machine Gun Company,
Army Form C. 2118.

WAR DIARY
or
INTELLIGENCE SUMMARY.
(Erase heading not required.)

Place	Date 1917	Hour	Summary of Events and Information	Remarks and references to Appendices
TRENCHES	July 14	10pm to 12-30am	9 machine guns of the company cooperated in putting up a machine gun barrage on GAVRELLE SUPPORT TRENCH in I 2 a, whilst a raid was being made by the 17th Division on WHIP TRENCH at I 2 c 1.5. In all 1500 rounds were fired.	Ref FRANCE Sheet 51b NW 1/20,000
			5 O.R. Reinforcements joined the company from M.G.C. Base depot.	
	15th		Uneventful.	
	16th		The Divisional General Major General LAWRIE, C.B., D.S.O., visited the machine gun position in the Brigade sector. Inter-platoon Relief took place.	Appendix No 5
	17th 18th		Uneventful. 1 O.R. Killed in action. 2 O.R. Wounded	
	19th		4 O.R. Reinforcements joined the company from M.G.C. Base depot.	
	20th	1am to 2am	In conjunction with a raid which was carried out on GAVRELLE TRENCH from C 25 a.9.4. to C 25 b.3.0. by 2 companies of the HOWE Battalion, 12 machine guns were used. During the progress of the raid the trenches on the flanks were swept by machine gun fire in order to prevent the enemy either opening fire on	

188th Machine Gun Company.

Army Form C. 2118.

WAR DIARY
or
INTELLIGENCE SUMMARY.
(Erase heading not required.)

Place	Date 1917	Hour	Summary of Events and Information	Remarks and references to Appendices
TRENCHES	July 20		Our raiding party on attempting to advance his own line. 8 guns were used to do this & on each flank of the raid and then fire in cooperation with that of Stokes Mortars and Lewis guns proved to be most successful as no enemy machine guns opened fire during the raid. 4 guns assisted by guns of the Machine Gun Company on the left put a machine gun barrage on SOUTH GAVRELLE TRENCH from C.26.c.5.3. to C.26.c.7.7. About 200 additional cartridges containing about 60 gallons of Burning oil were also fired on SOUTH GAVRELLE TRENCH as well as thermite Bombs from trench mortars. The raid was most successful, 11 prisoners of the 128 I.R. 36th division being captured. Enemy retaliation for the raid was fairly heavy, a strong barrage being put up on our front and support lines during the raid. In all a total of 27,500 rounds were fired by our machine guns during and after the raid. 2 OR wounded in action.	Ref FRANCE Sheet 51bNW. 1/20000

188th Machine Gun Company
Army Form C. 2118.

WAR DIARY
or
INTELLIGENCE SUMMARY.
(Erase heading not required.)

Place	Date	Hour	Summary of Events and Information	Remarks and references to Appendices
TRENCHES	1917 July 21st		2 Lieut. E. LIGHT joined the company from M.G.C. Base depot.	Ok.
	22nd		Inter Section Relief	see Appendix M6
	23/25		Uneventful.	

During the past three weeks the company carried out a very extensive programme of night firing. In all about 170,000 rounds were fired principally with the object of harassing the enemy's communications. On nights when enemy reliefs were suspected to be taking place particular attention was paid to junctions of tracks and places which were centres of activity, such as headquarters. The firing was carried out both with the Artillery and without the normal number of guns which was employed was six. These guns were rifled from the Support and Reserve line positions. There is no doubt that nightly firing by machine guns on various targets behind the enemy lines has a certain moral effect on the enemy. Even although the machine gun bullets may not hit more than a man or two occasionally, the fact that the enemy

188th Machine Gun Company.
Army Form C. 2118.

WAR DIARY
or
INTELLIGENCE SUMMARY
(Erase heading not required.)

Place	Date	Hour	Summary of Events and Information	Remarks and references to Appendices
TRENCHES	July 25th 1917		Know that a place is likely to be swept by M.G. fire he ho a certain effect upon them especially men engaged in tasks such as carrying parties. Ration parties and digging parties. A prisoner of the 9th Company 28th Inf. Regt. 36th division who was captured in the raid of the 19th/20th July. stated in his examination that he knew of several casualties having been incurred through M.G. fire on back areas and also testified to the excellence of the M.G. Barrage put up on the night of the raid on GAVRELLE SUPPORT TRENCH in co-operation with the artillery barrage and barbing oil barrage.	
"	26th "		6 O.R. reinforcements joined the company from M.G. Corps Base Depot	K.
"	27th "		2/Lt E H JONES returned from M.G. Course at CAMIERS.	K.
"	28th "	7 am	Lt J LIGHTBODY left to go on a course at the G.H.Q. S. Army School, Machine Gun Branch.	Appx
"	28th "	8 pm	2/Lt J. McLAREN wounded on action. Inter Section relief	Appx Appx No
"	29 "		Unsuccessful. Received copy of 188 Inf. Brigade Order No 131 with	Appx. 7 Appx Appx

188th Machine Gun Coy.
Army Form C. 2118.

WAR DIARY
or
INTELLIGENCE SUMMARY.
(Erase heading not required.)

Place	Date	Hour	Summary of Events and Information	Remarks and references to Appendices
TRENCHES	1917 July 29		reference to the relief of the 188 Brigade by the 189 Brigade on the nights of July 30/31 st & July 31 st/Aug. 1 st.	Staff
"	30		Issued Relief Order No 8 to all concerned. 188th Bdge relieved Appen. 8. by the 189th Brigade.	Staff
"	31		Received news that the 2nd, 5th & 1st French Army had made an attack on the YPRES sector, the 5th & 1st French Army taking the second objectives along the whole front & the 2nd Army reaching the first objective. Relieved in the evening by the 189 M.G. Coy.	Staff

T.2134. Wt. W708—776. 500000. 4/15. Sir J. C. & S.

WAR DIARY — NO. 188 MACHINE GUN COMPANY. — Appendix No. 3

OPERATION ORDER No 3.   July 3rd. 1917.

1. The 188th. Machine Gun Company will relieve the 94th. Machine Gun Company in the right sub-sector of the Divisional front on the night 4/5th. July.

2. Distribution as per attached table.

3. All trench stores, aeroplane photographs and information regarding the tactical situation will be taken over on relief. Receipts for trench stores and maps to be forwarded to Company H. Q. by first runner.

4. (a). COMMUNICATIONS. 1 runner will be attached to each of Nos. 1, 3 & 4 Sections. He will go up with the O. C. Section on relief to reconnoitre the route and will return to Company H. Q. next morning by 7-0 a.m. These men will then form Headquarters Runners.

   (b). CHAIN OF COMMUNICATION. The front line runner will take any messages he has to the support line runner, who will in turn take the messages to Advanced Company H. Q., whence they will be sent by runner or 'phone to Company H. Q.

5. Box Respirators will be worn in the "alert" position during relief.

6. Belt boxes and tripods will be taken over at all the gun positions.

7. ANTI-AIRCRAFT SIGHTS. 2 A.A. Sights will be taken over at the Red line positions and at Company H. Q. These should be included on the list of trench stores.

8. RETURNS. Will be rendered to Company H. Q. by Section Officers at the usual times while in the line.

9. "RELIEF COMPLETE" will be reported to Company H. Q. through the outgoing Section Officers.

10. USE OF TELEPHONE. Attention is drawn to the extreme care which is needed when using the telephone, especially when in forward positions. All messages should be sent in the Company Code.

11. NUMBER OF MEN PER GUNTEAM IN THE LINE :-
    4 per gunteam in the front line.
    5 "   "   "   "   support line.
    4 "   "   "   "   Red Line.
    The above figures are exclusive of Corporals or Sergeants.

12. Company will parade at 5-30 p.m. and move to Transport Lines. Dress :- Fighting Order. 2 pairs of socks per man to be carried in haversack, also iron rations & knife, fork and spoon. Mess tin will be slung outside haversack. No greatcoats will be carried. Packs will be dumped at Coy. H.Q. by 2-0 p.m. tomorrow, 4/7/17.

(Signed.) J. Lightbody, Lt. & Adjt.
188th. Machine Gun Company.

RELIEF TABLE.

SECTION.	OFFICER I/C.	POSITION TO BE RELIEVED.	TIME OF PARADE.
No. 4.	2/Lt. Griffiths.	4 front line guns; 1, 2, 3 & 4 positions.	
No. 1.	2/Lt. Cooke.	Support Guns 5, 6, 7 & 8.	
No. 3.	2/Lt. Sidwell.	9 & 10, Red Line.	
No. 2.	2/Lt. McLaren.	2 guns in reserve at Coy. H.Q.	

Issued to all concerned.

War Diary
Appendix No 4

NO. 188 MACHINE GUN COMPANY.

SECRET

OPERATION ORDER NO. 4.

July 7th 1917

There will be an Inter-Section Relief on the night of Tuesday, 10th./11th. July.

RELIEF will be carried out in accordance with Relief Table appended.

BOX RESPIRATORS will be worn in the "ALERT" position during Relief.

All Trench Maps on charge of the Position will be handed over to the relieving Officer.

GUNS and SPARE PARTS will not be handed over.

COMPLETION OF RELIEF will be reported to Company H. Q. by wire, and the following code words will be used :- "JOHNNY WALKER."

Rations on Tuesday evening will be drawn by the teams about to be relieved for the relieving teams.

Section Officers will render a return of Ration Strengths for NEW Positions by 6-0 p.m. Monday, 9th. inst.

(Signed.) J. Lightbody, Lt. & Adjt.
188th. Machine Gun Company.

RELIEF TABLE.

GUN POSITIONS.	OFFICER NOW IN CHARGE.	RELIEVING OFFICER.	SECTION NOW HOLDING.	RELIEVING SECTION.	REMARKS.
9 & 10.	2/Lt.Sidwell.	2/Lt.Griffiths.	No. 3 (2 teams)	No. 2 (2 teams)	2 teams No. 2 leave Coy.H.Q. at 8-30 p.m. a limber will be provided for guns to be at Coy.H.Q. by 8-0 p.m.
5,6,7 & 8.	2/Lt.Cooke.	2/Lt.Sidwell.	No. 1 (4 teams)	No. 3 (4 teams)	2 teams No. 3 Leave Coy.H.Q. as above.
1,2,3 & 4.	2/Lt.Griffiths.	2/Lt.Cooke.	No. 4 (4 teams)	No. 1 (4 teams)	
RESERVE.	-	-	No. 3 (2 teams) No. 2 (4 teams)	No. 2 (2 teams) No. 4 (4 teams)	

Relief to commence at 8-30 p.m. with Nos. 9 & 10 positions, and thereafter will be progressive. Half limber will be at advanced Coy. H. Q. Ration Dump at 2-0 a.m. 11th. inst to take down guns of No. 4 Section to Coy. H. Q. This limber will leave Ration Dump at 2-30 a.m., even if guns have not all arrived.

Issued to all concerned.

J. Lightbody Lt. & Adjt.
188th M.G. Coy

WAR DIARY Appendix No 5.

No.186 M.G.COY. OPERATION ORDER No.5.

SECRET.

Ref. sheet 51bN.W.
TRENCH MAP.   18th. July 1917.

There will be an Inter section relief tonight.
Relief will be carried out in accordance with relief table appended.
BOX RESPIRATORS will be worn in the ALERT position during relief.
All trench maps in charge of the position will be handed over to the
relieving officer together with all information regarding the situation
GUNS and SPARE PARTS will not be handed over.
RATIONS tonight will be drawn by the teams about to be relieved for the
relieving teams, and handed over on relief.

RELIEF TABLE

GUN POSITIONS	OFFICER NOW IN CHARGE	RELIEVING OFFICER	SECTION NOW HOLDING	RELIEVING SECTION	REMARKS.
9,10,11, 12.	2/Lieut. McLaren.	2/Lieut. Griffiths	No. 2.	No. 4.	4 teams h.q. & leave Coy. H.Q. at 8.30.p.m. 2 Number will be provided to take guns to ADV. H.Q.
5,6,7,& 8.	2/Lieut. Stilwell.	2/Lieut. McLaren.	No. 3.	No. 2.	
1,2,3,& 4.	2/Lieut. Cooke.	2/Lieut. Stilwell.	No. 4.	No. 3.	
RESERVE.	2/Lieut. Griffiths.	2/Lieut. Cooke.	No. 4.	No. 1.	

RELIEF to commence at 8.30.p.m. with Nos. 9,10,11,&12 positions....
and thereafter will be progressive, each Section when relieved
Coy.H.Q. at 2.0.a.m. 17th. Less to 1.k. telephones at Coy. Headquarters
Coy. H.Q. This number will be under orders .... Headquarters Coy.
H.Q., even if they have not been relieved.

Acknowledge receipt.

to H.Q. 4. M. I.   ....Lt. & Adjt.
                                                                186th. Machine Gun Company.

Appendix No. 6.

SECRET   NO. 188th. MACHINE GUN COMPANY OPERATION ORDER NO.6

COPY NO. 1

Ref. Trench Map Sheet 51BN.W. 1/20,000
Secret Map SUGAR FACTORY 1/10,000

20th. JULY 1917

(1). There will be an inter section relief on the night of the 21/22nd. July.

(2). The relief will be carried out in accordance with attached table.

(3). BOX RESPIRATORS will be worn in the ALERT position during relief.

(4). All trench maps on charge of the position will be handed over to the relieving officer together with all information regarding the situation.

(5). GUNS and SPARE PARTS will not be handed over.

(6). RATIONS for the night 21/22nd. will be drawn by the teams about to be relieved for the relieving teams, and handed over on relief.

(6a). SECTION OFFICERS will render a return to coy. H.Q. by 1st. runner on Saturday 21st. July, giving Ration strengths for their new positions.

RELIEF TABLE.

Gun Positions.	Officer now in charge.	Relieving Officer.	Section now holding.	Relieving Section.	Remarks.
1=2=3=4.	2/Lieut. SIDWELL.	2/Lieut. McLAREN.	No. 3.	No. 2.	These guns are now re-numbered nos. 4,5,12, and WINDMILL Gun.
5=6=7=8.	2/Lieut. McLAREN.	2/Lieut. GRIFFITHS.	No. 2.	No. 4.	These guns are now re-numbered nos. 13,15,16,17.
RED LINE 9=10=11 &12.	2/LIEUT. GRIFFITHS.	2/Lieut. COOKE.	No. 4.	No. 4.	4 teams of no. 4 section leave coy. H.Q. at 8.30 p.m. A limber will be provided to be at coy. H.Q. by 8.15 p.m. to take these guns to top of TOWY TRENCH, where they will unload and proceed to their positions.
RESERVE	2/Lieut. COOKE	2/Lieut. SIDWELL.	No. 1.	No. 3.	1/2 limber will be at Advanced COY. H.Q. at 2.0. a.m. 22nd. inst. to take guns of no.3 section to Coy. H.Q.

Relief will commence at 8.30. p.m., and will be progressive. i.e., RED" SUPPORT, and FRONT LINES in that order.

ACKNOWLEDGE.
COPY no 1.....WAR DIARY
     2..... do.
     3.....2/Lieut. SIDWELL.
     4.....2/Lieut. McLAREN.
     5.....2/Lieut. GRIFFITHS.
     6.....2/Lieut. COOKE.
     7.....Transport Officer.
     8.....O.C. Company.

..........LT. &ADJT.
188th. M.G. Company.

SECRET   188th. M.G.Coy. ORDER NO. 7.   *Appendix No 4*

Ref. sheet 51 B.N.W. 1/2 [...]   28th. July 1917.
                                                          War Diary

There will be an inter section relief [...]

The relief will be carried out in [...]
BOX RESPIRATORS will be worn in the alert position on the [...]
AMMUNITION [...]

REQUESTS for TRENCH STORES [...]   Coy. H.Q.
by 1st. Section by the 29th. [...]
GUNS and SPARE PARTS will not be handed over.
RATIONS for the night of the 28/29th. will be drawn by the [...]
to the relieved section, excluding bacon, which [...]
A REPORT, giving particulars that the relief positions has [...]
[...] Coy. H.Q. by 1.30 a.m. on 29th. [...]

RELIEF TABLE.

Gun Positions	Outgoing	Incoming	Remarks
[...]	[...]	[...]	No. 3 section leave camp [...]
			at 8.45 p.m. [...]
			Two trucks, [...] will unload at [...]
[...]	[...]	[...]	[...]
1,2,3, [...]	[...]	[...]	[...]
24.	No.3 [...]	[...]	[...]
RESERVE M.G.	[...]	No. 3 section Coy. H.Q. [...]
	the guns of No. 3 section at Coy. H.Q.		
Relief will [...]			

2 [...]

Somebody H.Q. adjt.
188 M.G.Coy

SECRET   RELIEF ORDER No.8.   COPY No. 1

Appendix 8

by
Captain J.B.JONES D.S.C.
Commanding 188th. Machine Gun Company.

War Diary

(1) (1) The 188th. Machine Gun Company will be relieved by the 189th. Machine Gun Company on the night of July 31st./Aug. 1st.
(2) On completion of relief the Company will be located at WEST ROCLINCOURT CAMP (A 28 Central)
(3) ALL Trench Stores, Aeroplane Photographs, Documents and Maps giving dispositions and work being done in the Sections commanded by Section Officers will be handed over to Relieving Sections and Receipts obtained. The following will be the procedure for the handing over of Trench Stores:-
   (a) Each Section Officer will make out in triplicate a list of Trench Stores for each Gun Position. He will give these lists to the N.C.O. in charge of Position who will have them signed by Relieving N.C.O. He will give one copy to the Relieving N/CO,and the other two copies to his Section Officer who will hand them in to Company H.Q.
   (b) Regarding Trench Maps only these will be handed direct by Section Officers and a receipt obtained from the Relieving Officer.
(4) Gas Helmets will be worn in the "Alert" position during relief.
(5) Transport Lines and Q.M. Stores will remain in their present location.
(6) RELIEF GUIDES. One Guide per Section will report at Company H.Q. at 7p.m. on the 31st.inst.
The Guide for the RED LINE Guns will conduct his relieving Section to Advanced Company H.Q. where he will be met by guides from each Gun Position. SUPPORT LINE Guide will conduct relieving Section to the Junction of TOWEY ALLEY and NAVAL TRENCH where they will be met by Guides from each Gun Position.
FRONT LINE Guide will conduct relieving Section to No. 4 Position where he will be met by Guides from each Gun Position.
2/Lt. Sidwell will remain at ADVANCED COMPANY H.Q. Gun Teams,after relief, will proceed independently to Company H.Q. reporting at Advanced H.Q.on their way down. Section Officers will also report there and ascertain from Lt.Sidwell if all their teams have passed . Lt. Sidwell will remain there until the last Gun Team has reported, when he will telephone , "Relief complete" using code word "DUNHILL".
SIGNALLERS in advanced stations,after being relieved will attach themselves to the next Gun Team returning to Company H.Q. On arrival at billets, they will report themselves to the Signalling Corporal.
Tea will be provided for Sections at Company H.Q.
The reserve Section and Headquarters Staff will proceed to billets immediately after relief.
Sections will proceed under Section Officers from Company H.Q.to Transport Lines where they will meet guides who will conduct them to their billets.
(7) TRANSPORT. One limber will be at Company H.Q. at 3p.m.and will be at the disposal of Headquarters until relief is complete.
A half limber will be at Advanced Company H.Q. at 10p.m. to take Red Line Guns and Advanced Company H.Q. Stores.
One limber will be at Advanced Company H.Q.at 1 a.m. to take Support and Front Line Guns. 2/Lt. Cooke will detail two men to guard the Guns of his Section at Advanced Coy.H.Q. they will pack the limber and return with it after the arrival of Front Line Guns
(8) Tripods and belt boxes will be handed over ALL OTHER Gun equipment including Very pistols, perescopes, A.A.Sights, T shaped bases, Clinometers &c will be brought away.
Petrol tins,3 per Gun Team and 2 per Section H.Q. will be handed over & a receipt obtained on the Trench Stores List.

ACKNOWLEDGE.

Copies to
1 & 2 War Diary
3 Office
4/7
8 T.O.

E.Hugh Jones 2/Lt. Capt.
Commanding 188 Machine Gun Coy. M.G.C.

Confidential

Headquarters
186th Machine Gun Coy

Vol 16 1917

WAR DIARY

of

188th Machine Gun Company

From

1st Aug. 1917
to
1917

Volume No 4 will Appen. Nos g. 10, 11, 12 & 13.

To Officer i/c Records
Machine Gun Corps

O.C.
Comdg. 188th Machine Gun Coy

188th Machine Gun Company
Army Form C. 2118.

WAR DIARY
or
INTELLIGENCE SUMMARY.
(Erase heading not required.)

Instructions regarding War Diaries and Intelligence Summaries are contained in F. S. Regs., Part II. and the Staff Manual respectively. Title pages will be prepared in manuscript.

Place	Date 1917	Hour	Summary of Events and Information	Remarks and references to Appendices
WEST ROCLINCOURT CAMP	Aug 1	12.30am	Relief completed. Company moved in camp at WEST ROCLINCOURT. During the tour of duty on the trenches, which lasted 28 days, the company was very active. 250,000 rounds were expended on night firing on German communication trenches, tracks, ration dumps & strong points besides participating in a raid made by the 188th Bde. & layings by means of a barrage a raid made by the 179th I.R. on our right. Three Boches were dug in the support line & ours had to be moved running out to them. Our casualties were light. Key consisted of 1 Officer wounded, 1 O.R. killed 2 & O.R wounded. The relay system of runners adopted was found to be very satisfactory.	
"	" 2		However	Apx
"	" 3		Lt. T.C. LOW & 2/Lt. F. ROBERTSON joined the Coy from M.G.C. Base Depot. Received copy of 188th Brigade Order No 132, with reference to the relief of the 188th Bde by the 188th Bde between 7/8 Aug.	Apx

188th Machine Gun Coy

Army Form C. 2118.

WAR DIARY
or
INTELLIGENCE SUMMARY.
(Erase heading not required.)

Place	Date 1917	Hour	Summary of Events and Information	Remarks and references to Appendices
WEST ROCLINCOURT CAMP	Aug 4		Training.	
"	5		1 Off. & 15 O.R. detailed to attend Entr'army Special Church Parade Service near HOUDAIN, to commemorate the beginning of the 4th year of the War.	Off.
"	6/7		Training. Relief Orders issued to all concerned on the 6th.	Off. See Off. 9
"	8	12 noon	Left WEST ROCLINCOURT CAMP to relieve 189 th M.G. Coy in the line	
TRENCHES	"	5 pm	Relief complete. No alteration had taken place in the position of the guns held by H.2. to now in the line plus formerly used as advanced Coy H.Q. at H.4. a.3.5.90. Maj. Ref. Point do Jour 1/10000. The same system of communication, which worked so well the last time in the line, was again adopted. The sections were located as follows- Front Line. No 1. Section under 2/LT COOKE, Suffolk Line No 3 Section under 2/LT SIDWELL RED LINE No 2 Section under LT LOW & No 4 Section under 2/LT GRIFFITHS in reserve at Coy H.Q.	2 Off.

188th Machine Gun Coy
Army Form C. 2118.

WAR DIARY
or
INTELLIGENCE SUMMARY.
(Erase heading not required.)

Place	Date 1917	Hour	Summary of Events and Information	Remarks and references to Appendices
TRENCHES	Aug 9		Uneventful.	Appx
"	12		Quiet & uneventful.	Appx
"	13		Inter-section relief.	Appx 10
"	14	1am	Instructions were received from the D.M.G.O. that support line guns were to bar barrage lines of fire & to be laid on their SOS lines every night.	Appx
"	15		News received that the barracks lofts on our left had made an attack NW of LENS & captured all their objectives. 2/Lt W. FITZGERALD returned from leave on the OR. 2/Lt COOKE proceeded on a 5 days course with C Battery of the 223 Bde RFA to learn arbitrary methods of barrage.	Appx
"	16		News received that the 1st FRENCH Army & the 5th British Army had made an attack between STIRLING CASTLE & BIXSCHOOTE. Later richer relief. 20 OR joined the company, 5 from each Batt in 21st Brigade.	Appx 11

T2134. Wt. W708—776. 500000. 4/15. Sir J. C. & S.

188th Machine Gun Coy

WAR DIARY
or
INTELLIGENCE SUMMARY
(Erase heading not required.)

Army Form C. 2118.

Instructions regarding War Diaries and Intelligence Summaries are contained in F. S. Regs., Part II. and the Staff Manual respectively. Title pages will be prepared in manuscript.

Place	Date Aug/17	Hour	Summary of Events and Information	Remarks and references to Appendices
Trenches	17th/18		Uneventful	Sgd
"	19 "		Capt J. B. DODGE & 1 O.R. proceeded on leave to the U.K. 2/Lt CROFT returned from Artillery course & 2/Lt ROBERTSON proceeded on artillery course.	Sgd
"	20"		1 O.R. proceeded to ORVILLE on a 6 weeks advanced signalling course. Instructions received from Brigade to move Coy H.Q. to its former position and H.1 & 7.4. Inter-section relief.	Sgd 4212 Sgd
"	21"		Coy H.Q. moved to dug-outs in H.1 & 7.4. Advanced Coy H.Q. was established at R1 position. Brigade Order No 136 received regarding the relief of the 188 th Inf Bde by the 189 th Inf Bde on the night of Aug 24/25 & the 188 MG Coy by the Lt 189 M.G. Coy on the night of Aug 25/26 st.	Sgd
"	22nd		Uneventful	Sgd
"	23rd		2/Lt ROBERTSON returned from Artillery Course & 2/Lt LIGHT proceeded on the same course.	Sgd

WAR DIARY
or
INTELLIGENCE SUMMARY.

(Erase heading not required.)

Army Form C. 2118.

188 L Machine Gun Coy.

Place	Date	Hour	Summary of Events and Information	Remarks and references to Appendices
Trenches	Aug 24th		188 L Inf Bde relieved by the 189 Inf Bde. Operation Order No. 3 issued to all concerned.	Self
"WEST ROSSINCOURT" CAMP	25th		Relieved by the 189 L Machine Gun Coy. Relief complete.	Self
	26th		During the 1st days the Coy. were in its hut there were no casualties. A good deal of work was put in by the company on the safe on the support line & the positions generally entrenched. Enemy tracks & ration dumps were fired on every night & information obtained from a deserter showed that the enemy sustained more casualties by parties in this sector suffered more casualties by machine gun fire than by shellery fire.	
	27th		LT. J. LIGHTBODY returned from Machine Gun Course at CAMIERS. 2/LT LIGHT returned from shellery course & 2/LT GRIFFITHS proceeded on same course.	Self
"	28/29th		Training. Brigade Order 137 received regarding the	

Army Form C. 2118.

188th Machine Gun Coy.

WAR DIARY
or
INTELLIGENCE SUMMARY.
(Erase heading not required.)

Instructions regarding War Diaries and Intelligence Summaries are contained in F.S. Regs., Part II. and the Staff Manual respectively. Title pages will be prepared in manuscript.

Place	Date	Hour	Summary of Events and Information	Remarks and references to Appendices
WEST ROCLINCOURT CAMP	Aug 17 29			
	30		relief of the 189th Inf. Bde. by the 188 Inf. Bde. 2/Lt J. COOKE proceeded to CAMIERS on a Machine gun course.	
"	30			
"	31		Capt. J.B. DODGE returned from leave in the U.K. 2/Lt R.R. SIDWELL proceeded on an Artillery course & 2/Lt GRIFFITHS returned from Artillery course.	

SECRET.   188 Machine Gun Company. Appendix 9.   Copy No. 1
WAR DIARY   RELIEF ORDER No. 9.   Aug. 7th. 1917.

(1) The 188th. Machine Gun Coy. will relieve the 189th. Machine Gun Coy.
    in the Right Sub-sector of the Divisional Front on the 8th. August
    by 5-0 p.m.
(2) Distribution will be as per attached Table.
(3) All Trench Stores (including Petrol Tins) Aeroplane photographs,
    and information regarding the tactical situation will be taken
    over on relief. Receipts for Trench Stores and Maps to be forwarded
    to Coy. H. Q. by 9-0 a.m. on the 9thh. inst.
(4) Box Respirators will be worn in the "Alert" position during the
    relief and throughout the Company's tour of duty in the line.
(5) Belt boxes and Tripods will be taken over at all the gun positions.
(6) Returns will be rendered by Section Officers to Coy. H. Q. at the
    usual times.
(7) Extreme care must be exercised when using the telephone, especially
    in forward positions.   ALL messages should be sent in Coy. Code.
(8) RELIEF COMPLETE.   The Section Officer in charge of front line
    guns will report relief complete by runner to Support Line H. Q.
    Section Officer in Support will telephone relief complete to Coy.
    H. Q. for his Section and the front line Section by using Code
    word "DUNHILL".   Section Officer in charge of Red Line guns
    will report relief complete to Coy. H. Q. by runner.
(9) Auxiliary mountings will be fixed on the guns and each gun team
    will take a periscope in the line.
(10) ACKNOWLEDGE.
Copies to:-
1&2 War Diary.
3 Coy Office.   (Signed) E.Hugh Jones. 2/Lt. and a/Adj.
4-7=Nos. 1-4 Section Officers.   188th. Machine Gun Company.
 8 Transport Officer.

                        RELIEF TABLE.

Section.	Officer in charge	Position to be relieved.	Time of Parade
1.	2/Lt. Cooke.	4 front line guns 1,2,3&4 positions.	Leave bridge over railway (near Brigade H.Q at 2-0 p.m.
3.	2/Lt. Sidwell.	4 Support line guns S1,S2,S3&S4 positions	As above at 2-15 p.m.
2.	2/Lt. Light. (R1 dugout)	4 Red line guns R1,R2,R3&R4 positions	As above at 2-30 p.m.
4	2/Lt Griffiths.	4 guns in reserve.	

One limber will be at the disposal of Nos. 1 &3 Sections, it will
accompany No. 1 Section to the entrance to TOWEY TRENCH, after
No. 1 Section have taken their equipment, and it will await the
arrival of No. 3 Section.
One limber will be at the disposal of Nos. 2 &4 Sections, and will
work in a similar manner.

SECRET.   No 188 Machine Gun Company.   Copy No. 1

Operation Order No. 10.
----

(1) There will be an Inter-Section Relief on the night of Sunday Aug. 12/13th.
(2) The relief will be carried out in accordance with the appended Table.
(3) Box respirators will be worn in the "Alert" position during relief.
(4) All Trench maps, together with all information regarding the positions will be handed over to the relieving Officer.
(5) Guns and Spare Parts will **NOT** be handed over.
(6) Rations on the night of the relief will be drawn by the teams to be relieved, and handed over.

Acknowledge

RELIEF TABLE.

Gun positions.	Officer now in charge.	Relieving Officer.	Section to be relieved.	Relieving Section.	Remarks.
R1, R2, R3 & R4.	Lt. Low & 2/Lt. Light.	2/Lt. Griffiths	No. 2.	No. 4.	No. 4 Section will leave Coy.H.Q. at 8-30 p.m.
S1, S2, S3 & S4.	2/Lt. Sidwell. & 2/Lt. Robertson	Lt. Low. & 2/Lt. Light.	No. 3.	No. 2.	
1=2=3&4.	2/Lt. ~~Cooks~~ Cooke.	2/Lt. Sidwell & 2/Lt Robertson	No. 1.	No. 3.	
Reserve.	2/Lt. Griffiths	2/Lt. Cooke	No. 4.	No. 1.	

Copies to:-
    1 & 2   War Diary.
    3   Coy. Office.
    4-7   Nos. 1-4 Sections.
    8   Transport Officer.   (Signed) E. Hugh Jones. 2/Lt. &a/Adj

188 Machine Gun Company.

SECRET.   No. 188 Machine Gun Company.   Copy No. 1

OPERATION ORDER NO. 11.

(1) There will be an Inter-Section relief on the night of August 16/17.
(2) The relief will be carried out in accordance with the appended Table.
(3) Box Respirators will be worn in the "Alert" position during relief.
(4) All Trench maps together with all information regarding the positions will be handed over to the relieving Officer.
(5) Guns and Spare parts will NOT be handed over.
(6) Rations on the night of the relief will be drawn by the teams to be relieved and handed over.
(7) ACKNOWLEDGE.

RELIEF TABLE.

Gun position.	Officer now in charge.	Relieving Officer.	Section to be relieved	Relieving Section	Remarks.
R1a, R1, R2, R3.	2/Lt. Fitzgerald.	2/Lt. Griffiths.	No. 4.	No. 1.	No. 2 will leave Coy. H.Q. at 8-30 p.m.
S1, S2, S3 & S4.	Lt. Low & 2/Lt. Light.	2/Lt. Fitzgerald.	No. 2.	No. 4.	
1, 2, 3 & 4.	2/Lt. Sidwell & 2/Lt. Robertson.	Lt. Low & 2/Lt. Light.	No. 3.	No. 2.	
Reserve.	2/Lt. Griffiths.	2/Lt. Sidwell & 2/Lt. Robertson.	No. 1.	No. 3.	

Copies to :-

    1 & 2.   War Diary.
    3.   Coy. Office.
    4-7.   Nos. 1-4 Sections.
    8.   Transport Officer.

(Signed) E. Hugh Jones. 2/Lt. & a/Adj

188 Machine Gun Company.

SECRET. NO. 188 MACHINE GUN COMPANY. COPY NO. 1

44.12
War Diary

OPERATION ORDER NO. 12.

(1). There will be an inter-section relief on the night of August 20th./21st.

(2). The relief will be carried out in accordance with attached Table.

(3). Box Respirators will be worn in the "alert" position during relief.

(4). All trench maps, together with all information concerning the positions, will be handed over to the relieving Officer.

(5). Guns and spare parts will not be handed over.

(6). Rations on the night of the relief will be drawn by the teams to be relieved and handed over.

(7). Section Officers will visit the positions they are to take over during the previous day. 2/Lt. Fitzgerald will visit 2/Lt. Light during the morning; and 2/Lt. Griffiths will visit 2/Lt. Fitzgerald during the afternoon.

(8). ACKNOWLEDGE.

RELIEF TABLE.

GUN POSITIONS.	OFFICER NOW IN CHARGE.	RELIEVING OFFICER.	SECTION TO BE RELIEVED.	RELIEVING SECTION.	REMARKS.
R1a, R1, R2 & R3.	2/Lt. Cooke.	2/Lt. Sidwell.	No.1	No.3	2 teams of No.3 will relieve R1a & R1 at 6pm; other 2 teams will relieve at 8-30 p.m.
S1, S2, S3, & S4.	2/Lt. Fitzgerald.	2/Lt. Cooke.	No.4	No.1	Teams from R1a & R1 will relieve S1 & S2 at 7 p.m.
1, 2, 3 & 4.	2/Lt. Light.	2/Lt. Fitzgerald.	No.2	No.4	Teams from S1 and S2 will relieve Nos. 2 and 3 guns.
RESERVE.	2/Lt. Sidwell.	2/Lt. Light.	No.3	No.2	

(Signed.) E. Hugh Jones, 2/Lt. & a/Adjt.
188th. Machine Gun Company.

Copies to -
1 & 2. War Diary.
3. Coy. Office.
4 - 7. 1/4 Sections.
8. Transport Officer.

SECRET.　　　　　NO. 188 MACHINE GUN COMPANY.　　　COPY NO. 1

OPERATION ORDER NO. 13.

1. The 188th. Machine Gun Company will be relieved by the 189th. Machine Gun Company on the night of the 25th. inst.

2. GUIDES from all Gun Positions and Section Headquarters, including the two reserve guns in the RED LINE, will be at the steps to the GUNPITS (late Company Headquarters) in TOWY ALLEY at the following times :-

    From Front & Support Lines　　--　　7-30 p.m.
    From Red Line　　　　　　　　　--　　8-30 p.m.

3. 2/Lieut. Robertson will be at the Steps.
    He will supervise the apportioning of the Guides and will see that no unnecessary exposure takes place.

4. Tripods and Ammunition Boxes will be handed over to the incoming Company. Ammunition Boxes will be handed over <u>full</u>.

5. All trench stores, maps, range cards, order boards, defence schemes and aeroplane photographs will be handed over on relief. Trench stores include all petrol tins at the gun positions at the time of relief. Receipts for stores will be handed in to Company Office before 9-0 a.m. on the 26th. inst.

6. Limbers will be at Company Headquarters at the following times :-

    1 limber at 8-30 p.m.
    2 limbers at 9-0 p.m.

7. Teams will report at Company Headquarters as they are relieved, and will move off from there in sections to Camp at ROCLINCOURT.

　　　　　　　　　　　　　　　　..................., for Captain.
　　　　　　　　　　　　　　Commanding 188th. Machine Gun Company.

Copies issued to all concerned.

Confidential

Headquarters 18th Machine Gun Co
91/17
1/14/17

War Diary
of
18th Machine Gun Company

From Sept 1st 1917 to Sept 30th 1917

J B Hodge
Captain
Commanding 18 F Machine Gun Co

Army Form C2118

188th Machine Gun Company

WAR DIARY
or
~~INTELLIGENCE SUMMARY~~
(Erase heading not required.)

Instructions regarding War Diaries and Intelligence Summaries are contained in F.S. Regs, Part II. and the Staff Manual respectively. Title pages will be prepared in manuscript.

Place	Date	Hour	Summary of Events and Information	Remarks and references to Appendices
ROCLINCOURT.	Sept 1st	—	Uneventful	Ref Map 51 B N.W. & 1/20000
"	2nd	9am	The Company moved from divisional reserve at ROCLINCOURT and moved up to relieve the 189th Machine Gun Company in the right Brigade (GAVRELLE) sector. 12 gun positions were taken over from 189th Coy and 4 gun positions S5 & S6 and R5 & R6 were taken over from 190 M.G. Coy. The 188th Inf. Bde was also taking over more ground on its left flank in accordance with the extension of the divisional front. The dispositions of the Company on completion of relief were :— 1 gun in the front line System also 3 Mobile Battery guns two of which were employed to engage day targets with indirect fire 6 guns in Support and 6 guns in the RED, or Reserve line.	"A"
TRENCHES.	3rd to 6th	2pm	Relief completed. Uneventful. Very little hostile artillery activity. Enemy trench mortars became rather more active than usual.	

Army Form C. 2118.

188th Machine Gun Company

WAR DIARY
or
INTELLIGENCE SUMMARY.
(Erase heading not required.)

Instructions regarding War Diaries and Intelligence Summaries are contained in F. S. Regs., Part II. and the Staff Manual respectively. Title pages will be prepared in manuscript.

Place	Date	Hour	Summary of Events and Information	Remarks and references to Appendices
Trenches	Sept 7th	9.45 p.m.	The ANSON Battalion 188th Bde. carried out a raid on an enemy position at C 25 b. Machine Guns cooperated by sweeping the enemy trench on the flanks of the Raid with direct fire. Machine Gun batteries firing from our support lines, put up a Barrage on WIDE TRENCH. In this they were assisted by 4 guns from the Brigade on our right (19th Division). The Raid was successful the prisoners being taken had identification obtained. Enemy retaliation was very slight.	Ref map FRANCE Sheet 51BNW 1/20,000
do	8th	10pm	A Raid was carried out by the Brigade on our immediate right. 3 prisoners were captured.	J.
do	9th		A successful daylight shoot was carried out on various points behind the enemy lines, tracks etc. Observation was obtained in some cases.	J.
do	10th	4pm	8 guns (2 Sections) of the 223rd M.G. Coy relieved 8 guns of 188th M.G. Coy in the RED LINE and Support lines. Nos 1 and 4 Sections on completion of Relief moved to rest billets	

Army Form C. 2118.

188th Machine Gun Company.

WAR DIARY
or
INTELLIGENCE SUMMARY.
(Erase heading not required.)

Place	Date	Hour	Summary of Events and Information	Remarks and references to Appendices
Trenches	Sept 10th		In ST. AUBIN, where they came under the orders of the 223rd M.G. Coy for training purposes.	'B' Jr.
do	11th		Lieut T.C. LOW proceeded to England on leave. 1 O.R. Killed in action. 1 O.R. died self inflicted wounds.	R.
do	12th		2/Lieut F. ROBERTSON proceeded to Field Ambulance, Sick. A Daylight firing Programme was carried out.	R.
	13th 14th 15th		Uneventful	R.
do	16th	9 pm	Lt E.H. JONES and Lt W. FITZGERALD proceeded on leave to PARIS. A Raid was carried out on our right by troops at MONCHY LE PREUX. This drew very heavy retaliation on GAVRELLE.	R.
		12 Mid	A raid was carried out by the Brigade of the 17th Division on our immediate right. 4 prisoners and 2 machine guns were captured.	

Army Form C. 2118.

188th Machine Gun Company

WAR DIARY
or
INTELLIGENCE SUMMARY
(Erase heading not required.)

Instructions regarding War Diaries and Intelligence Summaries are contained in F. S. Regs., Part II. and the Staff Manual respectively. Title pages will be prepared in manuscript.

Place	Date	Hour	Summary of Events and Information	Remarks and references to Appendices
Lenches	Sept 17th		Uneventful.	
	18th		"	
	19th	7pm	The company was relieved by the 189th Machine Gun Company. The 2 sections of the 223rd M.G. Coy on completion of relief moved to ROCLINCOURT to rejoin that company. Nos. 2 & 3 sections, after relief, moved by light railway to ST AUBIN. During this period (Sept 2nd to Sept 19th) the enemy activity was much below normal. Our machine guns here very active both by day and night. All night firing was coordinated with the artillery programme and units of nothing was two obtained by harassing fire on the enemys communications. A successful programme of daylight firing was also carried out when weather conditions (visibility etc) were favourable. Registration was obtained in several cases.	"C"
ST. AUBIN	20th 21st		Uneventful. Reorganisation and preparation for move. 2/Lt. E.H. JONES and 2/Lt. W. FITZGERALD returned from PARIS.	

Army Form C. 2118.

188th Machine Gun Company

WAR DIARY
~~INTELLIGENCE SUMMARY~~
(Erase heading not required.)

Instructions regarding War Diaries and Intelligence Summaries are contained in F. S. Regs., Part II. and the Staff Manual respectively. Title pages will be prepared in manuscript.

Place	Date	Hour	Summary of Events and Information	Remarks and references to Appendices
ST. AUBIN	Sept 22nd	8 am	Company moved by motor Bus to billets in MONCHY-BRETON.	Ref Map LENS 11. 1/100,000. D
	23rd		Uneventful	
	24th		Training commenced.	
	25th		Lt T.C. LOW returned from leave.	
	25-29		Training - Part I + Part II fired on Range. Frontal Barrage by batteries of machine guns practised.	
	30th		Information received that Company will move very shortly. Preparation for move.	

SECRET.   NO. 188 MACHINE GUN COMPANY.   COPY NO.

OPERATION ORDER NO. 14.

1. The 188th. Machine Gun Company will relieve the 189th. Machine Gun Company on the 2nd. instant.

2. Tripods and ammunition boxes will be handed over by the 189th. Machine Gun Company.

3. The positions to be occupied by Sections are as follows :-
   No. 1 Section :- No. 2, No. 4, & 2 guns in Sunken Road.
   "   2   "   :- S5, S6, R5 and R6.
   "   3   "   :- S1, S2, S3 and S4.
   "   4   "   :- R1a, R1, R2 and R3.

4. Officers will be in the following Dug-outs :-
   No. 1 Section :- Right support Company Headquarters in "Willie" Support.
   "   2   "   :- Dug-out at S6.
   "   3   "   :- One Officer at Section Headquarters in Support Line & one Officer at S3 or S4.
   "   4   "   :- Dug-out at R2.

5. Telephones will be taken up by Nos. 1, 3 and 4 Sections.

6. Sections and Pack Mules will be ready to move off at the following times :-
   No. 1 Section - 9-30 a.m. (Two Mules.)
   "   3   "   & 2 guns of No. 2 Section - 9-40 a.m. (3 Mules.)
   "   4   "   & 2 "   "   " 2 Section - 9-50 a.m. (3 Mules.)
   Mules to be at Company Headquarters 15 minutes before starting time.

7. Guides will be at the junction of SUPPORT LINE and TOWY ALLEY to conduct the Guns for the SUNKEN ROAD into Positions.
   Other teams will not have guides.

8. Teams will move via the Duckboard Track and Towy Alley.

9. The guns at R5 & R6 will be under the orders of the Officer commanding the Section in the RED LINE.

10. TWO Runners will live in R1 Dugout, which will be the RELAY POST for all Runners to and from the line.

11. Limbers will report at Company Headquarters at 2-0 p.m. Headquarters will be ready to move off at 2-30 p.m.

12. Officers' Valises will be rolled and stacked outside the Mess by 9-0 a.m.

13. All "Packs" will be stacked at C.Q.M.S. Stores by 8-30 a.m.

(Signed.) J. B. Dodge, Captain.
Commanding 188th. Machine Gun Company.

Issued to all concerned.

SECRET.   NO. 188 MACHINE GUN COMPANY.

OPERATION ORDER NO. 18.

10.9.17.

1. The following Relief will be carried out on the night of the 10th./ 11th. September.

2. 8 gunteams from No. 223 Divisional Machine Gun Company will be attached to this Company for instruction.

3. These teams will occupy the 6 positions in the RED LINE and S5 & S6 positions in the Support Line.

4. The following table gives the order of relief :-

RELIEVING SECTION.	SECTION TO BE RELIEVED.
6 guns of No. 223 M. G. Coy.	No. 4 Section, and R5 & R6 of No. 2 Section.
2 " " " " " "	S5 & S6 of No. 2 Section.
R5 & R6 and S5 & S6 of No. 2 Section.	No. 1 Section.

No. 3 Section will remain as at present.

5. Lt. Lightbody will be in command of the FRONT LINE guns. Officers in the SUPPORT LINE will remain as they are. 2/Lt. Fitzgerald will be responsible for the teams in the RED LINE.

6. The teams for the RED LINE will leave these H.Q. at 6 p.m., and those for the SUPPORT LINE at 5 p.m.

7. No. 4 Section, No. 1 Section, and 2/Lt. Griffiths on relief will report to Company Headquarters and from thence will proceed to St. Aubin where they will be attached to No. 223 Company till further notice.

8. One full limber will be at Old Coy. H.Q. Dump (Gunpits) at 11 p.m. Teams as they are relieved will leave their guns and gun gear there, and one man in charge.

9. 2/Lt. Fitzgerald will remain for one night in the RED LINE, and will report on the 11th. September to Company Headquarters by 4-30 p.m.

(Signed.) T. Carfrae Low, Lt. & Adjt.,
188th. Machine Gun Company.

Issued to all concerned.

SECRET.   189th. MACHINE GUN COMPANY.   COPY NO. 8

OPERATION ORDER NO. 16.

1. The 189th. Machine Gun Company will relieve ½ the 188th. Machine Gun Company and ½ the 223rd. Machine Gun Company of all positions in the Right Brigade Sector on the 19th. inst.

2. On completion of relief the two sections of the 188th. Machine Gun Company will move to ST. AUBIN by train, leaving Chantecler at 11 p.m., 19th. inst.
   The two sections of the 223rd. Machine Gun Company will move to WEST ROCLINCOURT CAMP.

3. Small Box Respirators will be worn in the "alert" position during Relief.

4. Relief will commence at 3 p.m. No guides are required.

5. All Belt Boxes over 12 at each gun position will be returned with Rations to-night to the Transport Lines.

6. Two petrol tins per gunteam and per Section Headquarters will be handed over in the Support and Front line positions. The red line gunteams will bring out two petrol tins each and two for Section Headquarters. They will bring these to Company Headquarters. Lt. Brown will arrange to hand over to 189th. Machine Gun Company tomorrow, 14 petrol tins for which a receipt will be obtained.

7. Lt. Griffiths will arrange to take over the Billets occupied by 223rd. Machine Gun Company at ST. AUBIN. He will also arrange with the C.Q.M.S. for tea to be provided at 12-30 a.m. 20th. inst. for the two Sections arriving by train.

8. Q.M. Stores, Officers' valises, &c. will be moved to ST. AUBIN tomorrow morning. Move of Transport will be notified later. The Q.M.S. will arrange for tea to be provided at Company Headquarters from 8 p.m. onwards for men returning from the line.

9. On Relief, Section Officers will report at Company Headquarters.

10. Limbers will be required as follows :-
    (a). 1 limber at Company Headquarters at 6 p.m. to remove Office and Mess Boxes.
    (b). 1 limber at top of TOMY TRENCH at 7-30 p.m. to take guns of 223 Company to WEST ROCLINCOURT CAMP. Gun gear of 223 Company will be dumped here and a man left in charge if they come out before the limber arrives.
    (c). 1 limber at top of TOMY TRENCH at 8-0 p.m. to take guns &c. of Nos. 2 & 3 Sections to ST. AUBIN.

11. All trench maps and information with regard to work in progress will be handed over to relieving Officers. Receipts will be obtained for all trench stores, and these will be handed in to Company Headquarters by Section Officers after relief.

....(Signed.) J. Lightbody, Lt. & a/Adjt.
189th. Machine Gun Company.

Copy No. 1. 189th. M. G. Coy.   Copy No. 2. O i/c Red Line guns.
                                                   223 M. G. Coy.
  do.   3. 2/Lt. Sidwell.   do.   4. 2/Lt. Griffiths.
  do.   5. 2/Lt. Light.   do.   6. 2/Lt. Brown.
Copies Nos. 7 & 8 War Diary.

SECRET.

188th. Machine Gun Company
OPERATION ORDER No. 17

Copy. No. 2

Ref. Map
LENS 11
 1/10,000.

Coy. H.Q. 21/8/17.

I. The 188th. Infantry Brigade Group will move to the CHELERS area on the 22nd. inst.
II. The 188th. Machine Gun Company will move to MONCHY BRETON in accordance with para. 1.
III. The company will parade at 8.0. a.m. at Coy. H.Q. ready to embus.
IV. Transport will proceed by road on the morning of the 22nd. inst. under orders issued to the Transport Officer separately.
V. On arrival at the destination, the company will fall out and pile arms well clear of the road. Billeting party will report to the Staff Captain at the MAIRIE, MONCHY BRETON, after debussing.
VI. The following will be the Routine for the 22nd. inst...
Reveille...4.0.a.m. Parade at 5.45.a.m. in full marching order.
Breakfast...5.30.a.m.
VII. Rations for the 22nd. inst. will be carried on the man. These rations will be issued tonight.
Officers kits, cooks gear, etc., will be carried on a lorry.

Copies to
1.... WAR DIARY.
2....
3.... 2/Lt. Griffiths.
4.... 2/Lt. Light.
5.... 2/Lt. Bidwell.
6.... 2/Lt. Brown.
7.... O.C. Coy.
8.... C.Q.M.S.

............Capt.
O.C. 188th. M.G.Coy.

CONFIDENTIAL

188th Machine Gun Company

War Diary

Vol 18

181/(3)

From Oct 1st 1917

TO Oct 31/1917

E Bowditch Jr. Capt.
Commanding 188 M.G. Company.

WAR DIARY
or
INTELLIGENCE SUMMARY.
(Erase heading not required.)

Army Form C. 2118.

188 M E.654

Place	Date	Hour	Summary of Events and Information	Remarks and references to Appendices
MONCHY BRETON	1st Oct.		Preparation for move North.	yes
	2nd	9 AM	The Company marched from billets in MONCHY BRETON and entrained at TINQUES.	yes
		1:30 PM	Train No 2 containing the Company left TINQUES STATION.	
POPERINGHE			Company detrained at HOPOUTRE and marched to billets in POPERINGHE. A 30. Centre BELG. SHEET 28. N.W.	
DIRTY BUCKET CAMP.	3.		The Company marched to DIRTY BUCKET CAMP MAP reference A 30 Centre BELG. SHEET 28 N.W.	yes
	3-8		Uneventful - Company went into training	
"P" CAMP	9		Company moved to "P" CAMP-MAP Reference A 15. & 4.4	yes
	9-22		Company and carried out special training for attack. Pits were made so as to the best fighting dress for men going over the top. It was found best to put waterbottles & rations inside the pack which was slung on to the men's back by the trucking straps. This

Army Form C. 2118.

188 M G Coy

WAR DIARY
or
INTELLIGENCE SUMMARY.

(Erase heading not required.)

Place	Date	Hour	Summary of Events and Information	Remarks and references to Appendices
			was afterwards done in the attack & proved satisfactory. The haversack was found to be too small if more than 1 days ration was to be carried as well as the Iron Ration. As it was known that 8 guns would advance with the Infantry N°. 1 & 4 sections were detailed for this work & specialed for this purpose in their training. N°. 2 & 3 sections were trained for overhead barrage & were afterwards employed for this. During this time frequent visits were made to the line by O.C., Section Officers, N.C.O's & gun commanders and all ranks were made conversant with the position and prominent features were impressed on the men. By this means it was reckoned the chance of being direction was multiplied.	JBS

WAR DIARY

INTELLIGENCE SUMMARY
(Erase heading not required.)

Army Form C. 2118.

198 M.G. Coy

Place	Date	Hour	Summary of Events and Information	Remarks and references to Appendices
IRISH FARM.	23		Company marched to IRISH FARM CAMP. Map Reference C.27.a.2.7 28.N.W. Transport located at POTTEN FARM CAMP. Map reference It 3.0.-7.3 28 NW	JBX
	24		Company relieved 27th M.G. Coy. with in the sector South of POELCAPELLE with 8 guns (No 1 and 4 sections) No 2 & 3 sections went into the line and dug in on the positions chosen for frontal barrage fire. Officers with No 1 section 2nd Lt GRIFFITHS and 2nd Lt HAYES. Officers with No 4 section Lt JONES and 2nd Lt FITZGERALD. Officer with No 2 section No 4 section 2nd Lt JONES and 2nd Lt FITZGERALD. Officer with No 3 section 2nd Lt SIDWELL. 2nd Lt RIGHT and 2nd in charge of No 3 section. No. 2 & 3 sections formed half of a subgroup of 16 guns which was for contiguous frontal barrage under LIEUT. DENMHURST commanding 283 M.G. Coy.	JBX
	25.		Uneventful – zero hour for the 26th given as 5.40 A.M.	
	26.	3AM	No 1 and 4 sections were formed up for the tape by 3A.M. ZEROHOUR. No 1 Section on the Right supporting the AN'SON BATTN. with the HOWE BATTN. in rear (this last battalion being the leapfrogging battalion.) No 4 section on the Left supporting the 1st R.M.L.I. and the	

WAR DIARY or INTELLIGENCE SUMMARY

Army Form C. 2118.

188 M.G. Coy.

Place	Date	Hour	Summary of Events and Information	Remarks and references to Appendices
	26	5.40AM	2nd R.M.kl. in rear who were to dash frog & capture the 2nd Objective	JPD
			No 1 Section advanced 100 yds in rear of the first wave of Infantry and made for their objective viz VARLET FARM. 2 guns arrived within 50 yds of VARLET FARM and came into action and broke up a counter attack approaching from the left flank. One gun fired two belts & was then just out of action, the other gun fired 9 belts before being put out of action by a snipers bullet. This gun undoubtedly saved the situation. The remaining two guns owing to casualties never came into action.	
			No 2 Section advanced by gun teams to support of the Companies with whom they were to consolidate. Here guns succeeded in crossing the PADEBEEK & were remained there from 3 P.M. till about 7 P.M. until 8 rifles & guns were out of action. They then retired on BURNS HOUSE. The Infantry had previously retired owing to all rifles being jammed on account of the mud.	
			No 2 & 3 Sections fired according to the programme arranged by Div. G.O.	

WAR DIARY

INTELLIGENCE SUMMARY
(Erase heading not required.)

Army Form C. 2118.

188 M.G. Coy.

Place	Date	Hour	Summary of Events and Information	Remarks and references to Appendices
	26	10.30PM	No. 2 & 3 sections moved forward and relieved No. 1 & 4 sections disposition of guns 2 at COPSE HOUSE, 1 @ BURNS HOUSE, 2 at the CEMETRY North of WALLEMOLEN, 2 at INCH HOUSES	JBS
IRISH FARM CAMP	27		The Company was relieved by 189 M.G. Coy and moved to billets at IRISH FARM CAMP.	JBS
do.	28		Checked personnel & gear of Company. Total Casualties during 25th, 26th & 27th Officers 1 killed 2 Lt GOVES 1 wounded and evacuated 2 Lt SIDWELL, 2 wounded and remained at duty viz :- 2Lt FITZGERALD and 2 Lt HAYES. 10 Other Ranks killed 37 wounded 4 missing 2 wounded & remained at duty	JBS
do.	29-31		Company reorganised & refitted. A certain amount of gear was salvaged from the line. Lt LOW was in the line during these days assisting at GOLDINGHAM of 190 M.G.Coy in frontal barrage by Machine Guns in support of the offensive by the 190th Inf. Brigade.	JBS

J B Moore Capt
O.C. 188 M.G.Coy

SECRET

War Diary
166 M. Gun Company

Nov 1st 1917
" 30th "

From
To

Vol 19

Army Form C. 2118.

188 M.G. Coy

WAR DIARY
INTELLIGENCE SUMMARY.
(Erase heading not required.)

Place	Date	Hour	Summary of Events and Information	Remarks and references to Appendices
DAMBRE CAMP	1/Nov		Company moved to DAMBRE CAMP from IRISH FARM	9/25
	2nd		Reorganisation Baths Inspection by Divisional General on 4th Company entrained at DAMBRE CAMP and proceed to the line for the purpose of doing Barrage, 2 Sections doing Barrage, 2 Sections holding the line. It Fitzgerald was in charge of 4 guns (consolidating) on the left subsector Headquarters at the shaft V.27.a.05.45. He had 1 gun with him at H.2 & 3 guns in vicinity of Banff House V.27.B.5.5. 2/L Hayes was in command of Right consolidating guns H.2 at V.28 & 5.4. He had 2 guns with him at H.2 & 2 guns at V.28.c.3.6. It Row was in command of 8 Barrage guns situated at D.3.a.6.5.15. His H.2 were in a shell hole at D.2.d.9.8. Coy Headquarters at Hübner Farm. When Brigade Headquarters were	9/25 9/25

Army Form C. 2118.

WAR DIARY
or
INTELLIGENCE SUMMARY.
(Erase heading not required.)

1st M.G. Cy

Place	Date	Hour	Summary of Events and Information	Remarks and references to Appendices
Sm.	6th		At 6 a.m. Canadians attacked and Captured Passchendaele Ridge. PASSCHENDAELE — Our 8 Barrage Guns Cooperated by firing 30,000 rounds in the Vicinity of Vat Cottage D29 a.5.9.	gas

Army Form C. 2118.

WAR DIARY
or
INTELLIGENCE SUMMARY.
(Erase heading not required.)

188th M.I. Coy

Place	Date	Hour	Summary of Events and Information	Remarks and references to Appendices
IRISH FARM	Nov 7		Company came out at 12 A.M to IRISH FARM. Being Relieved by 216 Coy.	9RS
SCHOOL CAMP	8		" Left IRISH FARM by tram and were accommodated at SCHOOL CAMP	9RS
"	9		Sorted gun gear & equipment	9RS
"	10		Uneventful	9RS
"	11		"	9RS
WINNEZEELE	12	9 A-	Vacated SCHOOL CAMP & marched to WINNEZEELE & were accommodated in tents in the majors field	9RS
LEDRINGHAM	13	9 A-	Left WINNEZEELE & marched to LEDRINGHAM. R	9RS
"	14-20		Uneventful. Usual training carried out	9RS
"	21		Inspection by G.O.C 63rd Division	9RS
"	22-23		Uneventful	9RS
"	24-25		Inspection by Commander Buckhurst C.B. R.N. H.M.S Australia Sheet 26. B27.c.9.4.	9RS
"	25		Orders Received to move to DAMBRE CAMP on 26th Sheet 26. B27.c.9.4	9RS
DAMBRE CAMP	26	9 A-	Coy moved to DAMBRE CAMP by Bus arriving 1 P.M. Accommodated in tents. Attached to 32nd Division for a Barrage Scheme	9RS

Army Form C. 2118.

WAR DIARY
or
INTELLIGENCE SUMMARY.
(Erase heading not required.)

188th M.G. Coy

Place	Date	Hour	Summary of Events and Information	Remarks and references to Appendices
DAMBRE CAMP	27	2pm	Working party proceeded to D.4.d.8.9. (20 SE 3) to carry ammunition from KANSAS X Roads to gun position as above	JRS
"	28	2pm	Working party consisted of 40 men 1 officer 2/Lt Griffiths. Working party proceeded as above consisting of 1 officer 2/Lt WILLIAMS & 60 OR to carry & prepare emplacements	JRS
"	29	2pm	2/Lts Burns & Trifonlo taken up to position & Battery front posns. Remaining SAA stored up, working party as above	JRS
"	30	1pm	Company moved to IRISH FARM by train accommodated in tents IRISH FARM was shelled during this move. 1 casualty occurred	JRS
"	30	3pm	Company moved up the line under 2/Lt WILLIAMS 2/Lt HENSON 2/Lt SMITH & 2/Lt DODD with remainder of gun gear etc. Zero lines were laid out. Company located at IRISH FARM (Headquarters) AID UNused H.Q at D.4.d.9.7 (Ref m.f. 20 SE 3) TRANSPORT located at DAMBRE CAMP (Sheet 28 B 27.c.9.4).	JRS

T2134. Wt. W708-776. 500000. 4/15. Sir J.C. & S.

188 Inf Bde

188 Bde Diary
1st Oct to 31st Dec 1917.

Secret

WAR DIARY or INTELLIGENCE SUMMARY

Army Form C. 2118.

Place	Date	Hour	Summary of Events and Information	Remarks and references to Appendices
Line	Dec 1		Transports located at Dambre Camp Sheet 28 B27 & 96 Rues	
D4d79	2		A2 located at IRISH FARM. Uneventful	JJB
			The 97th Brigade attacked the enemy at 1.55 a.m. Our fire was no heavier at Zero + 8 than before & M.G. Barrage opened & carried on till Zero + 2 hours. During this Barrage "C" Battery was Situated at D.5.c. 3.5 and consisted of 7 guns under 2/Lt Henson & No 1 Sect. assisted by 2/Lt Smith. No 2 Sect fired 17000 Rounds. "D" Battery wh was Situated at D.5.c.2.5 and consisted of 7 guns under 2/Lt Williams & No 3 section assisted by 2/Lt DODD. No 4 Section fired 17000 Rounds. At 6 a.m. the Barrage was resumed for 2 hours. "C" Batty fired 17000 rounds "D" Battery fired 17250 rounds. During this Barrage "C" Batty Suffered - 1 killed Roomes & 1 Lt Steck. "D" Battery were opened SOS was sent up at 4.10 Bath Batterys	JJB

T2134. Wt. W708—776. 500000. 4/15. Sir J. C. & S.

WAR DIARY
or
INTELLIGENCE SUMMARY.
(Erase heading not required.)

Army Form C. 2118.

18th M.T. Cy

Place	Date	Hour	Summary of Events and Information	Remarks and references to Appendices
&c.	2		Opened fire "C" Batty fired 3600 rounds. "D" Batty fired 1225D rounds. Harassing fire was carried out during the day & night	JHB
	3		Returns were taken up to Coy Headquarters (advanced) at 7am from Irish Farm. Coy. H.Q. moved from the line at 5 pm arrived by 10 pm. two 8 h.o. a.k. a. camps party. Dinner was served at Sans Farm Coy H.Q. entrained for DAMBRE CAMP at 10 AM and were accommodated in tents	JHB
DAMBRE CAMP	4		Roll call, regrowals & sorting out & clearing of Guns arrivals	JHB
CAMP	5		Uneventful	JHB
Schools	6		Coy. moved by Road to Schools Camp during 11 a.m arriving	JHB
Camp P.	7		1.30 no casualties Accommodated in tents & Nissen Huts	JHB
	8		Inspected by D.M. 90. 63rd (RN) Division.	JHB
			Orders received to move. References for move Carried out	7

WAR DIARY
or
INTELLIGENCE SUMMARY.
(Erase heading not required.)

Army Form C. 2118.

188

Place	Date	Hour	Summary of Events and Information	Remarks and references to Appendices
	Dec.			
BEAULEN-COURT N.15.a	9th		Company entrained with transport at 8.43 a.m at PESTELHOEK & proceeded to ACHIET LE GRAND, detrained & marched to BEAULENCOURT CAMP (Australian Corps) & were accommodated in Nissen Huts at 11.45 a.m	7/B
"	10th		Location of Company & transport. N.18.a (Ref. map. ———— LENS.11)	7/B
"	11th		Company unofficially inspected by G.O.C. 155th Inf. Brigade	7/B
			Company unofficially inspected by G.O.C. 113th Inf. Brigade & D.M.G.O. who complimented it on its transport	7/B
"	12th		Unsuccessful, but for usual parades & cleaning of arms gear & ammunition overhaul.	7/B
"	13th		Unsuccessful, but for usual parades. Preparations for moving made	7/B
ROCQUIGNY	14th		Company moved by road to ROCQUIGNY at 2pm. & were accommodated in Nissen huts.	7/B
MANANCOURT	15th		Company moved by road at 10.20 a.m to MANANCOURT - & were accommodated in tents there	7/B
LECHELLE	16th		Company moved by road to LECHELLE at 10-25 a.m & were	7/B

WAR DIARY
or
INTELLIGENCE SUMMARY.
(Erase heading not required.)

Army Form C. 2118.

Place	Date	Hour	Summary of Events and Information	Remarks and references to Appendices
In the Line	25		Unidentified trail of occasional Shelling	JWB
	26		" " " "	JWB
	27		" " " "	JWB
	28		" " " Harassing fire carried out on Lt VACQUERIE	JWB
	29		Transport moved to E. EQUANCOURT	JWB
	30		Heavy enemy Barrage at 6.20. Enemy moved an attack from 2ND QUENTIN. Mr. of Barrage put up. 5000 Rounds fired. Deliverance Guns fired 2 Barrels (wounded.) Officers Reported not yet Shewed.	JWB
	31		Relief of all Sections carried out works by Wagons. Rover section moved to Front line i Ver Venow. In Shell was put close on Coy H.Q. located at A.19.a.10.c.5.R. in Reserve Lines also hvy Shelling the around taken	
			W.B. Lane	

Army Form C. 2118.

WAR DIARY
or
INTELLIGENCE SUMMARY.
(Erase heading not required.)

Instructions regarding War Diaries and Intelligence Summaries are contained in F.S. Regs., Part II. and the Staff Manual respectively. Title pages will be prepared in manuscript.

Place	Date	Hour	Summary of Events and Information	Remarks and references to Appendices
LECHELLE	Oct 16		accomodated in Nissen huts at the Machine Gun Camp	78D 78B
"	17		Uneventful except for usual parades. One officer was sent to make a reconnaissance of approaches & route to the line	78B
"	18		Uneventful except for usual parades. Message from General Schuler - G.O.C. 32nd Division, complimenting the Company on its work for his division on 1st December to 3rd December 1917 was read to the Coy. by C.O.	78B
"	19		Uneventful - except for usual parades.	78D 78B
"	20		Uneventful - except for usual parades	78B
"	21		Uneventful - except for usual parades	78B
METZ	22		Company moved by road to METZ - map reference Q.20 - C.10.90 - the transport located at P.6.6.7.2.	78B
"	23		METZ was bombed during interval. Coy commdr. carried out a Reconnaissance of the line & arrangements for Relief were made Transport located at FINS	78B
"	24		Relief was carried out with 189 M.G. Company & completed by 6 h.r. no casualties. 14 guns were put into position in 3 Posts commanded by Post I 2/Lt HAYES MC Post R1 2/Lt HENSON M.P. & Post R11 2/Lt WILLIAMS M.M.	78B

T2134. Wt. W708—776. 500000. 4/15. Sir J. C. & S.

Confidential

Vol 21

188 Coy M.G.C. War Diary
From 1st to 31st January 1918

WAR DIARY or INTELLIGENCE SUMMARY

Army Form C. 2118.

188 MG Coy

Place	Date	Hour	Summary of Events and Information	Remarks and references to Appendices
Anthuille Wood	1/7/18 Jan.		Coy in Hutts dropped in the neighbourhood of Fever Farm. Afternoon quiet.	A/A/A
	2.		Unusual(?)	A/A/A
	3.		Slight enemy artillery activity	A/A/A
	4.		Heavy shelling of VILLERS PROUCH down the evening (6pm-8pm) Remainder of the day quiet.	A/A/A
	5.		Relief which carried out during the morning into Company arrangement. I1 and R1 posts relieving Front line and Support posts.	A/A/A
	6.		Posts were before daybreak away to shelling of Line. Arranged at times in Company being in the line and two in reserve at METZ. Day quiet.	A/A/A
	7.		Guns in I1 and R1 posts fired on who SOS lines.	A/A/A
	8.		Harassing fire was carried out during the early morning (1-5am) by guns in R1 post; target being Road Junction GONNELIEU x R26 d. Also fire in Barrage (7½am-12 midnight) by I1 post, target Junction at R22c x R27 d. Relieved in the afternoon to R16 a Road Junction at 6pm.	A/A/A
	9.		Company relieved by 190 M. G. Coy. Relief complete by 6pm when the Company moved to Brigade Reserve and occupied the former billets at METZ.	
METZ	10.		Reorganisation of Company.	A/A/A

Army Form C. 2118.

WAR DIARY
or
INTELLIGENCE SUMMARY.
(Erase heading not required.)

188 M G Coy

Instructions regarding War Diaries and Intelligence Summaries are contained in F.S. Regs., Part II. and the Staff Manual respectively. Title pages will be prepared in manuscript.

Place	Date	Hour	Summary of Events and Information	Remarks and references to Appendices
METZ.	Jan 11		Inspection of Guns Van and KH.	
	12		Resuming of Gunning etc.	
	13-16		No Training. All available men working on METZ Defences.	3782
In the line	17		Company moved into line, relieving 190 Coy M.G.C. in left sub sector of Divisional front. Transport was broken at EQUANCOURT. The day passed without untoward incident	47
	18		Uneventful. All actions during an improving positions according to orders issued by Group Commander	47
	19		Uneventful - made key arrival on as above	47
	20		Uneventful - do	47
	21		Uneventful - do + Reconnoitre relief carried out	47
	22		Uneventful - do	47
	23		Uneventful - do	47
	24		Uneventful. The Company was relieved by 99 M.G. Coy relief being complete by 7.30 a.m. Sections marched off to EQUANCOURT independently. Hot tea being provided at METZ + hot dinner	24

Army Form C. 2118.

WAR DIARY
or
INTELLIGENCE SUMMARY.
(Erase heading not required.)

188 M G Coy.

Instructions regarding War Diaries and Intelligence Summaries are contained in F. S. Regs., Part II. and the Staff Manual respectively. Title pages will be prepared in manuscript.

Place	Date	Hour	Summary of Events and Information	Remarks and references to Appendices
EQUANCOURT	24		at EQUANCOURT. The Company stayed in billets overnight.	A
ROCQUIGNY	25		Company moved to ROCQUIGNY by rail. Transport moving by road. On arrival the Company was located in Arian Mission huts at O.27.d.7.9. There was bombing by hostile aircraft during the night, in which the Company suffered 1 killed & 4 wounded thereabouts. All company perfecting defences against bombing	A
	26		—do—	A
	27		—do—	A
	28		—do—	A
	29		—do—	A
	30		—do—	A
	31		—do—	A

Army Form C. 2118.

WAR DIARY
or
INTELLIGENCE SUMMARY.
(Erase heading not required.)

188 M G Coy

Vol 2

Place	Date	Hour	Summary of Events and Information	Remarks and references to Appendices
ROCQUIGNY	Feb 1st		The Company carried out further improvements to the Camp	
"	2		Transport inspected by Brigadier General & congratulated on the excellent appearance of men, animals & transport generally	Lt
"	3		Uneventful. Usual company training.	Lt
"	4th Sun			Lt
"	5		Preparations for demonstration of Barrage fire	Lt
"	6		Continuation of Preparations	
"	7		Usual parades in morning. Between 2 & 3 p.m. the Coy gave a demonstration illustrating action of Coy assisting infantry in attack. The Coy was divided into 2 - 8 gun batteries. The spectators witnessed the demonstration from (a) Battery Position - & 400 yds in front of Battery Position - & from within 50 yds of target.	Lt
			At 3 p.m the transport was inspected by Lt Col Riddle - A.S.C. O.C. 63rd Div. Train	Lt
			C.S.M Savage was this day awarded the Croix de Guerre - by H.M. The King of the Belgians in recognition of services rendered by him during the Company's tour of duty in Flanders	Lt

WAR DIARY
INTELLIGENCE SUMMARY

Army Form C. 2118.

1884. M.G.C.

Place	Date	Hour	Summary of Events and Information	Remarks and references to Appendices
Rocquigny	Feb.	8th	Uneventful — usual day training.	
"	"	9th	Uneventful — usual day training.	
"	"	10th	— Orient in the evening.	
"	"	11th	day spent by the Major	
"	"	12th	Anniversary of Armistice.	
"	"	13th	Coy leave Rocquigny for the Rear Head quarters, detail to return. Movement cancelled.	
Havrincourt Wood	"	14th	Coy first line in the uneventful	
"	"	15th	Infantry engaged in wire, expect rain yet	
"	"	16th	Uneventful by M.G. on German guns.	
"	"	17th	Details engaged. Bullets against Hotts trenching.	
"	"	18th	Uneventful	
"	"	19th 20th 21st	Two Stations came out of the line, were relieved by the 5th Coy	
"	"	22nd	Coy again Gun into the line in the left armour Scots, the 5 guns teams that remained, were withdrawn — ? with wiped pits no position	

Army Form C. 2118.

INTELLIGENCE SUMMARY

(Erase heading not required.)

188th M.G. Coy.

Place	Date	Hour	Summary of Events and Information	Remarks and references to Appendices
Hamricourt Wood	Feb.	23D. 24th 25th 26th 27th	Coys. woke in the line, experiencing a makein, no protaro [casualties] Relieved do do do Coy Headquarters were heavily shelled, bombardment lasted for 4 hours, one Barrage position suffered a direct hit, Gun Teams untouched, two men killed, one aircoup position blown in.	SR. SR. SR.
		28th	Bn's quiet, but were relieved by the 199 th M.G. Coy. proceeded to billets in the Machine Gun Camp neuville.	SR.

A5834 Wt. W4973 M687 750,000 8/16 D. D. & L. Ltd. Forms/C.2118/13.

www.ingramcontent.com/pod-product-compliance
Lightning Source LLC
Chambersburg PA
CBHW081433160426
43193CB00013B/2273